*The Rational Guide To*

# Building

# SharePoint
# Web Parts

**PUBLISHED BY**

**Rational Press** - An imprint of the Mann Publishing Group
208 Post Road, Suite 102
Greenland, NH 03840, USA
www.rationalpress.com
www.mannpublishing.com
+1 (603) 601-0325

ISBN: 0-9726888-6-2
Library of Congress Control Number (LCCN): 2004112370
Printed and bound in the United States of America.
10  9  8  7  6  5  4  3  2  1

**Trademarks**

**Disclaimer of Warranty**

**Credits**

| | |
|---|---|
| Author: | Darrin Bishop |
| Technical Editor: | Zac Woodall |
| Copy Editor: | Jeff Edman |
| Book Layout: | Molly Barnaby, Marcelo Paiva |
| Series Concept: | Anthony T. Mann |
| Cover Concept: | Marcelo Paiva |

# The Rational Guide To
# *Building*
# *SharePoint*
# *Web Parts*

*Darrin Bishop*

**RATIONAL PRESS**

An imprint of the
www.mannpublishing.com

# About the Author

Darrin Bishop is a Senior Technical Consultant in the Portal Group of a midwest consulting company. Darrin is a certified MCSD and focuses exclusively on designing and developing Microsoft SharePoint technology-based solutions. He has been working with SharePoint since the Beta 2 release of SharePoint Portal Server 2001 and is currently providing SharePoint design and development services to a variety of clients that maintain local and world-wide presences. When he is not actively engaged in SharePoint development, Darrin can be found evangelizing SharePoint and other Microsoft technologies throughout the midwest.

# Acknowledgements

I would like to thank the people who made this book possible:

Kurt Windisch, SQL Server guru, who matched up my idea for a book with Rational Press and convinced me that a book on Web Parts was needed.

Anthony Mann, who agreed to take on the project and also convinced me that a book on Web Parts was a worthwhile idea.

Zac Woodall, who provided the technical editing for the book and helped clarify concepts and ideas along the way. Zac really helped in understanding the Web Part infrastructure and how a Web Part ends up on the screen.

Greg Lindhorst, who provided much valuable information on Web Parts and Web Part development.

Jeff Edman, who, as a Mann Publishing Group editor, took the ramblings and technical jargon of a developer and transformed it into organized English for the reader.

The book could not have been possible if not for Betsy, Ben, and Meg, who did not complain about the late nights, phone calls, and missed outings. They supported the book from Day One. Without their support, the book would never have been completed.

 *Rational Guides for a*
*Fast-Paced World*™

# About Rational Guides

Rational Guides, from Rational Press, provide a no-nonsense approach to publishing based on both a practicality and price that make them rational. Rational Guides are compact books of fewer than 200 pages. Each Rational Guide is constructed with the highest quality writing and production materials — at a price of US$14.99 or less. All Rational Guides are intended to be as complete as possible within the 200-page size constraint. Furthermore, all Rational Guides come with bonus materials, such as additional chapters, applications, code, utilities, or other resources. To download these materials, just register your book at www.rationalpress.com. See the instruction page at the end of this book to find out how to register your book.

# Who Should Read This Book

This book explains what a Web Part is, how a Web Part participates in the web page, and how to develop custom Web Parts for your SharePoint Portal Server 2003 or Windows SharePoint Services installation. This book was written with .NET developers in mind, but it does not teach the reader how to develop software with Microsoft .NET technology. It is assumed that the reader has basic, working knowledge of the Microsoft .NET Framework, Visual Studio .NET, IIS, virtual servers, and some experience in developing web applications.

# Conventions Used In This Book

The following conventions are used throughout this book:

▶ *Italics* — First introduction of a term.

▶ **Bold** — Exact name of an item or object that appears on the computer screen, such as menus, buttons, dropdown lists, or links.

▶ `Mono-spaced text` — Used to show a Web URL address, computer language code, or expressions as you must exactly type them.

**Menu1**⇨**Menu2** — Hierarchical Windows menus in the order you must select them.

## Tech Tip:
This box gives you additional technical advice about the option, procedure, or step being explained in the chapter.

## Note:
This box gives you additional information to keep in mind as you read.

## FREE Bonus:
This box lists additional free materials or content available on the Web after you register your book at `www.rationalpress.com`.

## Caution
This box alerts you to special considerations or additional advice.

# Contents

# Contents

# *Introduction*

# Chapter 1

# Introduction to Web Parts

While information is key to any business, information alone is not enough: knowledge workers must be able to access, share, create, and modify information effectively in a team environment over a wide range of groups, applications, and data stores. Windows SharePoint Services and SharePoint Portal Server technologies provide a solid base for enabling teams to bring together people, processes and information.

As part of Windows Server 2003, Microsoft Windows SharePoint Services (WSS) allows you to create team-oriented sites for sharing resources and collaborating with other users on the team. Microsoft SharePoint Portal Server 2003 (SPS) is a separately licensed product that expands upon the "team" concept to allow additional capabilities such as personalized sites and single sign on. Both products work by displaying pieces of information in specific areas of the screen. These pieces are known as Web Parts. There are many standard Web Parts available from Microsoft, or you can develop your own for specific custom functionality. The Microsoft Web Parts are available from online galleries or may be installed with WSS and SPS 2003 into a local gallery of Web Parts.

Web Parts are a type of ASP .NET server control that plug into a web page hosted by either WSS or SPS. Web Parts expand on the ASP .NET server control base by providing a rich end-user experience, allowing users to customize a web page to their unique needs. Users with the appropriate security privileges can add, modify, and even remove Web Parts from their view of the web page without any developer customization. This rich user functionality is provided by the underlying ASP .NET Framework. The *Web Part infrastructure* is installed as part of WSS and includes the classes, functions, methods, and properties that render and process Web Parts. For more information on the Web Part infrastructure, see Chapter 3.

This chapter discusses Web Parts and the two applications that support them: Microsoft Windows SharePoint Services and Microsoft SharePoint Portal Server. After an overview of what a Web Part is and what it can do, we'll look at the WSS and SPS products that support Web Parts and discuss the differences between the current versions of these products and earlier versions.

Web Parts can be developed using any .NET-compliant language, such as Visual C# or Visual Basic .NET. With the support of the Web Part infrastructure, Web Parts can be modified, personalized, and connected.

Web Parts allow users to:

▶ **Modify** — Users can add, move, or remove Web Parts.

▶ **Personalize** — Users can change Web Part properties to display relevant information for the user.

▶ **Connect** — Users can connect Web Parts to each other to exchange information.

Web Parts provide developers with:

▶ **A familiar development environment** — Web Parts can be developed using any .NET-compliant language.

▶ **The .NET Framework** — Web Parts support data binding, Web Services, and the Common Language Runtime.

Web Parts provide server administrators with:

▶ **Security** — Administrators can control which Web Parts are allowed to run on their server and what resources a Web Part can access, such as Web Services or databases.

▶ **Management** —Administrators can manage Web Part properties and decide which Web Parts appear in galleries.

▶ **User configuration** —Web Parts allow the use of role-based access privileges. *Administrators* grant access to Web Parts on the server. *Designers* and *developers* create the sites. *Users* can modify and configure the Web Parts.

# What Can A Web Part Do?

A Web Part is an ASP .NET server control and can therefore do whatever a server control can do, but with added functionality. Web Parts emit HTML or XML that a web browser will use to display a web page. A Web Part lives on the server and is created for each HTTP request. Web Parts can participate in server-side events, connect to data sources, and maintain state. Practically any web-based application can end up as a Web Part.

Web Parts can help users do their jobs more quickly and easily, allowing them to keep track of critical information while doing their day-to-day work. A Web Part developer can create custom Web Parts to access information from a wide range of sources across an enterprise's infrastructure, including databases, network traffic reports, SPS indexing logs, or server event logs.

Database administrators, server administrators, and Help Desk users can use Web Parts to track important information. A database administrator can add Web Parts to display database information, while a SharePoint Portal Server administrator can add Web Parts to display summary index information.

Creating targeted web application functions or even an entire form-based application as a Web Part empowers end users to work from within a site or portal without continuously opening and closing multiple applications. For example, a Customer Service department might use a customer relationship management (CRM) application such as Microsoft CRM to access and update customer information. This same department might access a sales application like Microsoft Great Plains to access recent sales information. If they need information about an order shipment, they might access a database for shipping details, and then access the shipper's web site to determine where the order was delivered. A set of CRM Web Parts designed to display key customer information would be useful in this situation. Web Parts might be created to display sales information from the sales application. A shipping detail Web Part could display information from both the shipping details database and the shipper's Web Services. Connecting all these Web Parts will really make the solution shine. Connected Web Parts can feed information from one Web Part to another. The use of Web Parts allows the Customer Service department to have a page that provides essential information from multiple sources and systems in one location, with no need to open multiple applications for every service request.

Web Part solutions can benefit the entire organization as well as a single department. Web Parts are reusable across many different sites, and because the connections are generic, a Web Part can exchange information with other Web Parts. The CRM Web Parts described in the previous example might feed a **customerID** field to a Web Part that displays sales information in the Customer Service site. The same CRM Web Part might feed customer ID information to a sales management Web Part that will graph customer information over time.

Another use for Web Parts could be to access employee information stored in various back-end servers. Web Parts can display information such as payroll, health benefits, time off, and expenses. Administrators can choose to permit users to modify which Web Parts they want to see. For example, a user can have a payroll Web Part that is usually minimized and choose to look at it only on payday. If a user does not have health benefits, he can remove the health benefit Web Part from his view without affecting any other user's view of the Web Part. Let's look at how users can modify, personalize, and connect Web Parts.

## *Modify*

Web Parts can be modified in the following ways:

- ▶ Changing properties in the *tool pane*, a section of the screen which displays the Web Part properties as text boxes, dropdown lists, and check boxes.

- ▶ Dragging the Web Part to another location on the page.

- ▶ Selecting menu items from the Web Part menu.

All of these properties are modified in a web interface and require no resources from administrators or developers. Chapter 2 discusses how to modify Web Part properties.

## *Personalize*

End users can personalize Web Parts by modifying specifically designated properties marked for personalization by the Web Part developer. Personalizing a Web Part lets it use user-specific properties when rendering content. For example, a customer service Web Part can be created that allows a customer service representative to select a sales region to work with. Chapter 9 provides techniques for personalizing Web Parts.

## *Connect*

Web Parts can connect to each other when they implement complementary connection interfaces. Web Parts can implement provider and consumer interfaces. Changes in a *Provider Web Part* can cause a change in a connected *Consumer Web Part*. For example, an Image Web Part will display a specific image when a list item is selected in a connected List Web Part. Chapter 10 shows how to create connectable Web Parts.

# *Products Supporting Web Parts*

This book will only discuss Web Parts that are supported by Windows SharePoint Services 2.0 and SharePoint Portal Server 2003. WSS 2.0 is available as a download from Microsoft at

```
http://www.microsoft.com/downloads/details.aspx?FamilyId=E084D5CB-1161-
46F2-A363-8E0C2250D990&displaylang=en
```

Windows SharePoint Services 2.0 is considered part of the Windows Server 2003 platform and is licensed accordingly. SharePoint Portal Server 2003 is a Microsoft server product that requires server licenses and client access licenses.

## *Windows SharePoint Services 2.0*

Windows SharePoint Services 2.0 provides basic collaboration and document management functionality for teams. WSS 2.0 runs on Windows Server 2003, and is supported by Microsoft Internet Information Server (IIS), ASP .NET, and .NET Framework 1.1. SQL Server 2000 is the primary data store for WSS. Each virtual server can be provisioned to support one or more top-level sites. A top-level site can contain one or more subsites, each containing a collection of web pages, Web Parts, and child sites. For more information about WSS 2.0, visit:

```
http://www.microsoft.com/windowsserver2003/technologies/sharepoint/
default.mspx
```

Installing WSS 2.0 also installs the Web Part infrastructure, which contains .NET types, enumerations, and interfaces to support Web Parts. Web pages in a WSS site support all Web Parts placed in them with a SharePoint-aware HTML editor (such as FrontPage 2003), as well as those added to the underlying site definition. They also support Web Parts that end users add using a browser.

Figure 1.1 shows a basic Windows SharePoint Services site with the following Web Parts:

▶ Announcements

▶ Events

▶ Links

▶ WSS logo

**Figure 1.1:** Default Windows SharePoint Services Site.

## Microsoft SharePoint Portal Server 2003

Built on top of WSS 2.0, SharePoint Portal Server 2003 provides all WSS 2.0 functionality and adds categorization, indexing, content aggregation, user profiles, single sign on, and content targeting. SPS 2003 uses WSS 2.0 for core collaboration and document management. SPS 2003 uses and enhances WSS Sites for the portal user interface, and since it builds on WSS, it fully supports Web Parts. For more information about SPS 2003, see:

```
http://www.microsoft.com/office/sharepoint/prodinfo/default.mspx
```

Figure 1.2 shows an SPS home page with the following Web Parts:

▶ Links for You

▶ Portal Owner Quick Start Guide

▶ Group listings that display news

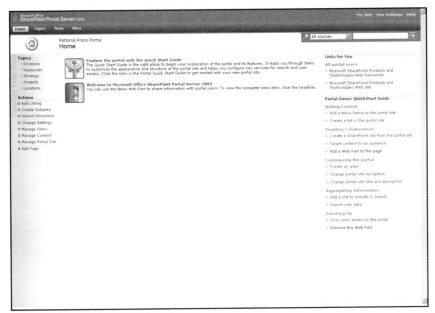

**Figure 1.2:** SharePoint Portal Server Home Page.

SPS 2003 pages may look different than pages in a WSS 2.0 site, but the portal pages are actually an extension of the WSS 2.0 site. SPS 2003 uses different site definition templates and Web Parts than WSS 2.0, but its core remains WSS 2.0. SPS 2003 is a superset of WSS 2.0, containing all WSS functionality, but adding more robust content searching, indexing, and user profiles. Because SPS 2003 uses WSS to render web pages, Web Parts that run on WSS 2.0 sites will also run on SPS 2003 sites.

*Tech Tip:*

Web Parts that run on an SPS 2003 site may not run on a WSS site. If the Web Part uses additional SPS 2003 functionality (such as user profiles), the Web Part may not be able to function correctly on a WSS 2.0 site.

## Browser Support

Internet Explorer 5.5 and later (on the Windows platform) provides the highest level of visual and functional support for Web Parts.

Internet Explorer 5.0.1 (with SP3) and Navigator 6.2 or later will support the majority of Web Part functionality on the Windows platform, but there may be some visual or functional inadequacy.

The UNIX and Macintosh versions of Navigator 6.1 and Internet Explorer 5.2 support even less functionality. Web Parts will still render data in these browsers, but the user experience will fall below that of the Windows browsers.

# Older Versions of Web Parts

Web Parts supported by WSS 2.0 and SPS 2003 are not the only Web Parts around. Earlier versions of Web Parts can be found in the Digital Dashboard Resource Kit (DDRK) and in the previous version of SharePoint Portal Server, SharePoint Portal Server 2001 (SPS 2001). The older versions are not compatible with the new versions. Web Parts developed for SPS 2001 are not supported on SPS 2003, and Web Parts developed for SPS 2003 are not supported on SPS 2001.

**Note:**

The Web Parts discussed in this book are intended to be used with WSS 2.0 and SPS 2003 — not with any older versions of these products.

There are some key differences between the older and newer types of Web Parts. The older Web Parts supported by SPS 2001 are script-based; they usually contain VBScript or JavaScript that runs on the server. This earlier version of Web Parts placed the script in the Web Part *definition file* (.dwp) right alongside the XML-serialized properties. Web Part code in SPS 2001 is easily copied and modified, and is interpreted rather than compiled. The serialized script is injected directly into the ASP page that renders the Digital Dashboard or SharePoint Workspace. This is a potential security risk, allowing users to upload code that can then run on the server.

The new Web Parts for WSS 2.0 and SPS 2003 are .NET assemblies created with any .NET-compliant language such as Visual Basic .NET or Visual C#. A *.NET assembly* is a unit of executable code that is managed by the Microsoft .NET Framework to provide optimized services during code execution. The Web Part definition file only details specific Web Part properties and information needed to locate the assembly, plus the actual Web Part class within the assembly. The code itself is not associated with the definition file but is built into the .NET assembly. End users can copy and exchange the definition file — which is just information about the specific Web Part — without exposing the underlying code.

Web Parts for WSS 2.0 and SPS 2003 are much more secure than their older, script-based predecessors. Unlike older versions of Web Parts, these new Web Parts are built with a .NET compiler, which compiles the intermediate language to machine code at runtime. Since these Web Parts are based on the .NET Framework, they participate in *Code Access Security* (CAS), which is a .NET security service to ensure that only permitted code will be able to run and access system resources. Server administrators can use CAS and *policy files* to modify privileges for the virtual server and assemblies. Limiting non-essential access to such system resources as the registry or file system reduces the possibility of malicious code doing damage (see Chapter 6 for more information). Additionally, the underlying Web Part infrastructure gives server administrators the final say over which Web Parts are permitted to run on the server, by allowing them to declare a Web Part as either safe to render or not safe to render. If someone adds a definition file to the site with a missing assembly or a Web Part that is not declared safe to render, it will simply fail to render.

# Development Environment Requirements

WSS 2.0 and SPS 2003 must be installed on a Windows 2003 Server. Neither will run on any prior versions of the Windows operating system, including Windows XP. Therefore, your *development environment* must include at least one server running Windows Server 2003.

Consider the following hardware configurations to be the minimum for developing effectively on both WSS 2.0 and SPS 2003:

▶ Processor: 700-MHZ

▶ Memory: 512 MB

▶ Hard Disk: 600 MB

For more information on setting up a development environment, see Chapter 4.

# Chapter 2

# Using Web Parts

This chapter shows how to add, modify, remove, and copy Web Parts, and gives you a brief tour of the *Web Part galleries*, where you will select the Web Parts for customizing your site. It also discusses the difference between personal and shared views, and describes how end users can personalize Web Parts.

The majority of procedures and examples in this chapter describe the use of Web Parts in Windows SharePoint Services (WSS) sites. For information on those areas in which SharePoint Portal Server (SPS) handles Web Parts differently than WSS, see the section "Using Web Parts with SharePoint Portal Server," later in this chapter.

## Note:

Although users usually have permissions to add, move, modify, and delete Web Parts, it is recommended for the examples in this chapter that you have site administrator privileges to avoid any permissions issues. For more information on roles and privileges, see the section "Site Group Privileges for Adding and Modifying Web Parts" later in this chapter.

# Adding Web Parts to a Web Part Page

Available Web Parts are contained in various galleries, which are visible in the tool pane on the right side of the screen in *design mode*. Design mode allows users to add, move, modify and delete Web Parts with drag-and-drop ease. Web Part galleries are available in the tool pane. Each gallery can contain Web Parts that users can drag and drop on to a Web Part page. Galleries can contain Web Parts distributed by Microsoft, Web Parts bought from a third party, Web Parts built by your IT department, or Web Parts customized by an end user and made available for others to use. You can use the tool pane to browse the Web Part galleries for the Web Parts you need. This is the most common way to locate Web Parts to add or modify.

The following procedure shows how to add an out-of-the box Web Part to a WSS or SPS page by choosing a new Web Part from a gallery in the tool pane:

1.  Open a WSS site based on the default **Team Site**, which is included with your WSS and SPS installation. The screen should look similar to Figure 2.1.

**Figure 2.1:** Basic Team Site in Windows SharePoint Services.

2.  In the upper right corner of the page, choose **Modify** ⇨ **Shared Page** ⇨ **Add Web Parts** ⇨ **Browse**. You are now in design mode. The tool pane opens on the right, allowing you to browse Web Parts in the Web Part galleries.

> ***Note:***
>
> If you see a **Modify My Page** menu instead of the **Modify Shared Page** menu, this means you are viewing the site in a Personal View instead of a Shared View. Choose **Modify My Page** ⇨ **Shared View** to switch to the Shared View. For information on views, see the section "Shared and Personal Views" later in this chapter.

Figure 2.2 shows the site with the tool pane open for browsing. You can tell that the Web Part page is in design mode because both the tool pane and the boxed Web Part zones are visible. *Web Part zones* are areas of the page where users can add or remove Web Parts. In Figure 2.2, the zones are labeled **Left** and **Right**.

**Figure 2.2:** Team Site with Tool Pane Open and Visible Web Part Zones.

3. Add a Web Part by dragging it from the tool pane onto a Web Part zone. For example, drag the **Members** Web Part from the **Browse** section of the tool pane and drop it below the **Links** Web Part, inside the zone titled **Right**. The **Members** Web Part should now exist inside the **Right** Web Part zone. Congratulations! You have just added your first Web Part.

4. Close the tool pane. The page will exit design mode.

Figure 2.3 displays the **Team Site** with the **Members** Web Part.

**Figure 2.3:** Team Site with Members Web Part.

*Note:*

If you are using a browser that does not support drag-and-drop functionality, you can still add a Web Part by using the **Add To** control and the **Add** button, as seen in Figure 2.2.

## *More Options for Adding Web Parts*

In addition to dragging Web Parts from the tool pane to Web Part zones, the following methods are available for adding Web Parts.

▶ **Search the galleries** — You can use the tool pane to search the galleries for the Web Parts you need. For information on searching Web Parts in galleries, see the section "Web Part Galleries" later in this chapter.

▶ **Use the Import Option to import Web Parts** — To add a Web Part that is not contained in a gallery, you must import its definition (.dwp) file from wherever the administrator has placed it on the server. Do this by choosing **Modify Shared Page** ⇨ **Add Web Parts** ⇨ **Import**. The imported .dwp will appear as an available Web Part in the tool pane's gallery. The .dwp file is a serialized XML document which represents a specific instance of a given Web Part control. It contains the information that allows the Web Part page to locate the required .NET assembly and type. It also contains basic information such as the Web Part title and description that will be displayed in the tool pane. The **Import** option only imports the definition file. It does not import any assembly or code. The assembly containing the Web Part must be installed and configured separately. For information on installing and configuring assemblies, see Chapter 11. The **Import** option never imports a .dwp file into the gallery permanently; as soon as you exit design mode, the Web Part will no longer appear in the tool pane unless you import it again.

*Note:*

Keep in mind that only users with sufficient access privileges will be able to import the .dwp file. Also, a Web Part control must be registered as safe before it can be rendered on the screen. For information on registering a Web Part as safe to render, see Chapter 4.

# Modifying Web Parts

End users can modify Web Part configuration at runtime simply by entering design mode and using the tool pane. There are many ways to modify a Web Part, but this section will explain one common way to do it. For more information on modifying Web Parts, refer to the "Working with Web Part Pages" section in the WSS and SPS Help files.

Use the following procedure to modify a Web Part:

1.  Open a WSS site based on the default **Team Site**, which is included with your WSS or SPS installation.

2.  In the upper right corner of the page, choose **Modify Shared Page** ⇨ **Modify Shared Web Parts** and select the Web Part to modify. You are now in design mode. The tool pane will display the available properties for the chosen Web Part. Figure 2.4 shows the **Modify Shared Web Parts** menu option.

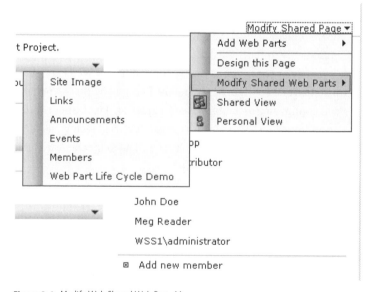

**Figure 2.4:** Modify Web Shared Web Parts Menu.

3. Make a change to a property and apply the changes. Applying changes will leave you in design mode with the tool pane available for more changes.

4. Click the **OK** button to close the tool pane. The web page will revert from design mode to view mode.

# Deleting Web Parts

Use the following procedure to delete a Web Part from a Web Part zone:

1. Open a WSS site based on the default **Team Site**, which is included with your WSS or SPS installation.

2. In the upper right corner, choose **Modify Shared Page** ⇨ **Modify Shared Web Parts**. You are now in design mode.

3. Click the down arrow on the Web Part title bar to select the Web Part menu. The Web Part Menu appears onscreen as a down arrow in the Web Part's title bar. If the Web Part does not have a visible title bar, make sure the Web Part page is in design mode.

4. From the **Web Part** menu, choose **Delete**.

> *Note:*
>
> Deleting a Web Part is not the same as closing a Web Part. Deleting a Web Part removes the Web Part from the Web Part zone. Closing a Web Part leaves the Web Part associated with the page, but no longer includes it on the page. Instead, closed Web Parts appear in the Web Part Page Gallery. For information on Web Part galleries, see the "Web Part Galleries" section later in this chapter.

# Copying Web Parts

You can also copy the settings of a particular Web Part and apply them to a different Web Part, by choosing **Modify Shared Page** ⇨ **Modify Shared Web Parts** and selecting the Web Part you want to export. From the Web Part menu, choose **Export**. This allows you to save a copy of the .dwp file to a local directory. You can import the .dwp file to another site or page. For more information on .dwp files, see Chapter 4.

**Note:**

Remember that the definition file is simply the serialized information of a specific instance of a Web Part. The **Export** function does not export the assembly that contains the Web Part class, nor does it register the Web Part as safe to render.

# Web Part Galleries

Web Part galleries are collections of Web Part definition (.dwp) files that are displayed in the tool pane. They represent configured, available Web Parts that you can place in Web Part zones on a web page. You can browse, filter, and search the galleries for the Web Parts you need.

## Finding Web Parts in Galleries

You can use the following methods to find available Web Parts in galleries:

▶ **Browse the galleries** — Choose **Modify Shared Page** ⇨ **Add Web Parts** ⇨ **Browse**. This is the procedure described in the section "Adding Web Parts to a Web Part Page" earlier in this chapter.

▶ **Search the galleries** — Choose **Modify Shared Page** ⇨ **Add Web Parts** ⇨ **Search**. Type your search criteria in the text box and click the **Go** button. This will search all the galleries for the **Title** and **Description** properties of the configured Web Part.

▶ **Use the Filter function** — This can be used for both browsing and searching. When browsing, click the **Filter** link in the tool pane and select a value to filter on. When searching, click the **Filter** link and select a filter value to apply to your found set.

Figure 2.5 shows the **Filter** list box from the **Browse** tool pane.

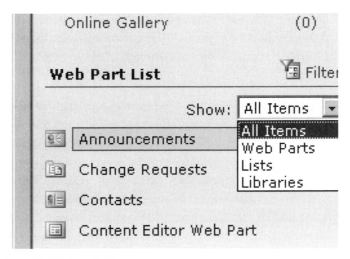

**Figure 2.5:** Filter List in Tool Pane.

## Types of Galleries

The tool pane allows you to access the following galleries:

▶ **<Site Name> Site Gallery** — This gallery contains Web Parts for the site collection and is prefixed by the site name. The Web Parts in this gallery are available to any Web Part page in the site collection. There is one site gallery per site collection. A *site collection* is the top-level site plus its subsites. A virtual server can have multiple site collections.

▶ **Virtual Server Gallery** — This gallery contains Web Parts that are available to any site collection hosted by the virtual server. There is one virtual server gallery per virtual server.

► **Online Gallery** — This remote gallery contains Web Parts that are available to all site collections on all virtual servers. Unlike the Virtual Server Gallery, the Online Gallery does not have to be hosted by the server on which the gallery is displayed. Each virtual server can be configured to point to a single Online Gallery using the `web.config` file. Administrators can create and host an Online Gallery and configure a SharePoint server to link to it. Administrators are responsible for configuring access to an Online Gallery. There can be only one Online Gallery per SPS or WSS server.

► **Web Part Page Gallery** — This is a unique gallery because does not contain new Web Parts to add to a page, but it still functions like any other gallery, allowing users to drag and drop Web Parts to Web Part zones. The Web Part Page Gallery contains Web Parts that have already been added to the page, but are closed. Closing a Web Part is not the same as deleting it. A closed Web Part remains associated with the page, but is no longer included on the page. A closed Web Part is no longer listed in the **Modify Shared Web Parts** submenu. The only way to access a closed Web Part is to browse the Web Part Page Gallery and drag the closed Web Part to a Web Part zone. There is one Web Part Page Gallery for each Web Part page.

When working with galleries, remember that they do not equate to working with code and assemblies. Galleries contain information about a specific configuration for a specific Web Part. The Web Part itself is actually code residing in an assembly which is available on the server. Galleries do not contain the Web Part code located in the assembly. Server administrators must add the assembly to the server and modify the `web.config` file before any instance of the Web Part can render. Chapter 11 shows how to install the definition file into galleries and add a Web Part to a page using a specific configuration.

Galleries also allow administrators to deploy a Web Part to a single gallery and make it available across many sites. For example, if a Web Part integrates with a Time Sheet or Payroll system, it is probably applicable to all employees. An administrator may choose to install this Web Part in the virtual server gallery so that it can be used in all virtual server sites and subsites. The job of adding Web Parts to galleries usually belongs to the administrator.

 *Caution:*

You cannot simply add a Web Part to a gallery and expect it to work. You must also install the assembly and mark the Web Part as safe to render. For information on marking a Web Part as safe to render, see Chapter 4. For information on installing assemblies, see Chapter 11.

## Installed Web Parts

WSS 2.0 and SPS 2003 install a set of basic Web Parts, which are added to the **<Site Name> Site Gallery**. By default, these basic Web Parts are marked as safe to render. Administrators can remove them as desired. Tables 2.1 and 2.2 show the installed Web Parts for WSS 2.0 and SPS 2003.

Table 2.1 shows the available Web Parts in a WSS 2.0 Virtual Server Gallery.

| WEB PART TITLE | DESCRIPTION |
|---|---|
| Announcements | This List Web Part displays announcements. |
| Contacts | This List Web Part displays contact information. |
| Content Editor | Contains text or HTML text for display. |
| Document Library | Allows storing and sharing of documents. |
| Events | This List Web Part displays event information. |
| Form Web Part | Web Part for HTML Forms. |
| General Discussion | Displays a discussion list. |
| Image Web Part | Displays images. |
| Links | This List Web Part displays links. |
| Members | Displays members of a site. |
| Page Viewer Web Part | Displays a web page. |
| Shared Documents Part | This Document Library Web Part allows documents to be shared with other team members. |
| Tasks | This List Web Part displays task list information. |
| XML Web Part | Displays XML information. |

**Table 2.1:** Available Web Parts in WSS 2.0 Team Site Gallery.

> ## Note:
> The Announcements, Contacts, Events, General Discussion, Links, Shared Documents, and Tasks Web Parts are available because the WSS Team Site template contains the associated lists and document libraries. WSS creates an associated Web Part for each list and document library.

Table 2.2 shows the available Web Parts in an SPS 2003 site gallery.

| WEB PART TITLE | DESCRIPTION |
|---|---|
| Area Content | This List Web Part displays sub areas. |
| Area Detail | Displays information about the area, such as owner. |
| Contacts | This List Web Part displays contact information. |
| Content Editor | Contains text or HTML text for display. |
| Document Library | Allows storing and sharing of documents. |
| Events | This List Web Part displays event information. |
| Form Web Part | Web Part for HTML Forms. |
| General Discussion | Displays a discussion list. |
| Group Listings | Displays listing (content) for an area. |
| Image Library | This Library Web Part stores images. |
| Image Web Part | Displays images. |
| Links | This List Web Part displays links. |
| Links For You | This List Web Part displays links. |
| My Alerts Summary | Displays links and alerts for a user. |
| My InBox | Displays a user's Exchange 2003 InBox. |
| My Links | This List Web Part displays a user's favorite links. |
| My Mail Folder | Displays a specified Exchange 2003 mail folder. |
| My Tasks | Displays a user's Exchange 2003 tasks. |
| My Workspace Sites | Displays a list of the user's workspaces created in the user's personal site. |
| News | Displays a news listing. |
| News Area | Displays news listings for any News sub areas. |
| News for You | Displays news listings targeted to the user. |
| Page Viewer Web Part | Displays a web page. |

| Topic Assistant Suggestions | Displays suggested topics information for an area. |
|---|---|
| Tasks | This List Web Part displays task list information. |
| XML Web Part | Displays XML information. |
| Your Recent Documents | Lists recent documents authored by the user. |

**Table 2.2:** Available Web Parts in SPS 2003 Site Gallery.

> *Note:*
>
> **The Contacts, Document Library, Events, General Discussion, Links, and Tasks Web Parts are available because SPS creates an associated Web Part for each list and document library.**

# Shared and Personal Views

Personalization allows users to customize their sites and Web Parts. One way to personalize a site is to allow each user to have a custom view of the site's pages. *Views* dictate what a particular user can see on a page. Views can be *Personal* or *Shared*.

> *Note:*
>
> **Shared and Personal Views refer to what a user sees on a Web Part page. This should not be confused with views related to a list or document library. Shared and Personal Views determine whether the user sees the same Web Part page as all other users, or if he sees a Web Part page modified for the specific user.**

## Shared Views

In a Shared View, all users will see the same layout and design. Anyone with read privileges can access a site's Shared View. The ability to modify a shared view is usually restricted to administrators and web designers, because any change to the Shared View will affect all users.

You can choose a specific view by selecting it from the **Modify Shared Page** or **Modify My Page** menus, as shown n Figure 2.6.

**Figure 2.6:** Selecting Shared or Personal View.

## *Personal Views*

In a Personal View, some design elements may be particular to a single user. Changes to a Personal View are only viewable by the user who makes the modification. This allows individuals to customize a site according to their needs. For example, a salesperson might add a Sales Page Viewer Web Part to the Sales site, in order to retrieve news about a particular client.

*Caution:*

Be careful when you modify WSS or SPS web pages. The ability to modify a Shared View should not be given to everyone. Modifications to a Personal View will not affect other users, but modifications to a Shared View certainly will. A user must not be allowed to inadvertently add a personalized Web Part to a Shared View, which could impose the personal setting of a single user on all users, or display incorrect or confidential information. To avoid making inadvertent changes to the Shared View of a web page, limit the number of users that have permissions to add and customize Web Pages. For more information on roles and privileges, see the section "Site Group Privileges for Adding and Modifying Web Parts" in this chapter.

# Site Group Privileges for Adding and Modifying Web Parts

WSS sites utilize role-based security, which assigns roles to users and groups. These roles are known as *site groups*, each of which is assigned zero or more privileges. WSS installs the following site groups:

▶ **Readers** — Not allowed to add, delete, or modify Web Parts, but they can still view and interact with the Web Part content on a Web Part page.

▶ **Contributors** — Allowed to add and remove Web Parts in the Personal View but not the Shared View.

▶ **Web Designers and Administrators** — Have the same personalization permissions as Contributors, but they may also add and customize Web Page privileges and modify the Shared Views that affect all users. Administrators can also create and modify site groups and their associated privileges.

To allow a user to personalize Web Parts, an Administrator simply adds the user to the **Contributor** site group. To allow the user to modify a Shared View, the user must be added to the **Web Designer** or **Administrator** site group. Another way to achieve this is to create a new site group with the **Add and Customize Web Pages** privilege and then add the user to the new site group. The best practice is to give each user the minimum amount of privileges required for their job.

You must have **Administrator** privileges to view and modify a site group's permissions. To access a site group's list of permissions, click the **Site Settings** link in the upper-right area of a WSS site. Select **Go To Site Administration** ⇨ **Manage Site Groups**. Choose a site group such as **Web Designer** and then select **Edit Site Group Permissions**. You will see a screen similar the one shown in Figure 2.7.

**Figure 2.7:** WSS Privileges for Web Designer Site Group.

The security and personalization features of SPS sites differ from those of WSS as described in the next section.

# Using Web Parts with SharePoint Portal Server

Up to this point, this chapter has been discussing Web Parts in Web Part pages hosted by a WSS site. Using Web Parts in an SPS environment differs from WSS in the following ways:

▶ **Accessing Design Mode** — To access design mode in an SPS 2003 site, you must select **Edit Page** from the left-hand navigation frame, as shown in Figure 2.8. The **Modify Shared Page** option will appear on the right-hand side. The remaining steps for adding, deleting, and modifying Web Parts are the same as in a WSS site. Selecting **View Page** from the left-hand navigation frame will return the portal to view mode.

**Figure 2.8:** Edit Page Navigation Link.

▶ **Targeting Content** — Targeted content is one of SPS 2003's big advantages over WSS. The majority of Web Parts that are installed with SPS are specific to a logged-on user. SPS 2003 installs a **Profile** database which can be populated and updated from Active Directory, and can therefore display information that is targeted to a particular user. For information on how custom Web Parts can utilize profile information, see Chapter 9.

▶ **Security** — WSS provides one set of roles per site, which means that a user who can modify Web Parts on one site page is allowed to do the same on all site pages. SPS 2003 allows administrators to add and remove a site group's access to each area. This means that a site group that is allowed to modify the Shared View in one area might not be allowed to modify the Shared View in another area.

▶ **Additional Site Groups** — SPS 2003 installs more site groups than WSS does, and allows different privileges. Administrators can create new site groups and assign privileges just as they do in WSS. SPS2003 installs the following site groups: **Reader**, **Contributor**, **Web Designer**, **Administrator**, **Content Manager**, and **Member**. The SPS default security settings assign the same permissions to Members, Content Managers, Web Designers, and Administrators that their WSS equivalents receive. In addition, SPS Web Designers and Administrators can add, remove, and update personalized Web Parts, as well as add and customize pages. Figure 2.9 shows the privileges available to SPS 2003 site groups.

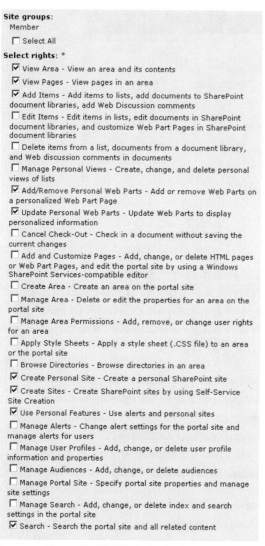

**Site groups:**
Member

☐ Select All

**Select rights:** *

☑ View Area - View an area and its contents

☑ View Pages - View pages in an area

☑ Add Items - Add items to lists, add documents to SharePoint document libraries, add Web Discussion comments

☐ Edit Items - Edit items in lists, edit documents in SharePoint document libraries, and customize Web Part Pages in SharePoint document libraries

☐ Delete items from a list, documents from a document library, and Web discussion comments in documents

☐ Manage Personal Views - Create, change, and delete personal views of lists

☑ Add/Remove Personal Web Parts - Add or remove Web Parts on a personalized Web Part Page

☑ Update Personal Web Parts - Update Web Parts to display personalized information

☐ Cancel Check-Out - Check in a document without saving the current changes

☐ Add and Customize Pages - Add, change, or delete HTML pages or Web Part Pages, and edit the portal site by using a Windows SharePoint Services-compatible editor

☐ Create Area - Create an area on the portal site

☐ Manage Area - Delete or edit the properties for an area on the portal site

☐ Manage Area Permissions - Add, remove, or change user rights for an area

☐ Apply Style Sheets - Apply a style sheet (.CSS file) to an area or the portal site

☐ Browse Directories - Browse directories in an area

☑ Create Personal Site - Create a personal SharePoint site

☑ Create Sites - Create SharePoint sites by using Self-Service Site Creation

☑ Use Personal Features - Use alerts and personal sites

☐ Manage Alerts - Change alert settings for the portal site and manage alerts for users

☐ Manage User Profiles - Add, change, or delete user profile information and properties

☐ Manage Audiences - Add, change, or delete audiences

☐ Manage Portal Site - Specify portal site properties and manage site settings

☐ Manage Search - Add, change, or delete index and search settings in the portal site

☑ Search - Search the portal site and all related content

**Figure 2.9:** Privileges for SPS 2003 Member Site Group.

# Chapter 3

# Web Part Infrastructure

Web Parts are based on ASP .NET server controls, but their additional functionality requires a supporting infrastructure in order to function. Without this framework, Web Parts cannot participate in generating web page output. The *Web Part infrastructure* contains the supporting code (classes, functions, methods and properties) needed to render and process Web Parts. It is installed with WSS 2.0, and is embedded in SPS 2003 as well. The Web Part infrastructure was specifically designed for use with WSS 2.0 and SPS 2003 and fully supports all Web Part features. This chapter describes the Web Part infrastructure and how it renders Web Part content to the page. It will also look at some of the .NET classes included in the Web Part infrastructure that developers can use to create custom Web Parts.

## *Web Part Infrastructure Overview*

The Web Part infrastructure is built on top of the ASP .NET Framework. Web Parts are in fact specialized ASP .NET server controls with added functionality, and Web Part pages are specialized ASP .NET pages that contain Web Parts.

The Web Part infrastructure provides:

►  **Reusable Components** — Like other ASP .NET server controls,
   Web Parts are reusable components. Web Part developers can create
   a single Web Part and use it one or more times in a single page or
   in different pages. The Web Part can also be deployed to multiple
   SharePoint sites and servers. For more information on deploying Web
   Parts, see Chapter 11.

▶ **Personalization** — The Web Part infrastructure allows a single Web Part to maintain shared settings as well as personal settings. A single Web Part can render content and functionality according to the user's privileges and needs without requiring the developer to write large amounts of code. For more information on personalizing Web Parts, see Chapter 9.

▶ **End-User Modification** — The Web Part infrastructure allows runtime property modification. A standard ASP .NET server control requires access to the `.aspx` file for any property modification. The Web Part infrastructure supports the modification of properties from the web browser. Not only can end users modify properties of Web Parts during runtime, they can also add and remove Web Parts using the web user interface. For more information on adding, modifying, and removing Web Parts, see Chapter 2.

▶ **Web Part Security** — The Web Part infrastructure enables administrators to use the `web.config` file to control which Web Parts and server controls are allowed to run on the server. A Web Part must be "allowed" to run before it can be rendered on a page. For more information on security, see Chapters 6 and 11.

▶ **Connectable Web Parts** — Web Parts can be connected on either the server side or client side through a known set of interfaces. The Web Part infrastructure defines the interfaces and methods for connecting Web Parts as providers and consumers. The Web Part infrastructure allows end users to create, modify and delete connections using web browsers. For more information on connecting Web Parts, see Chapter 10.

## How the Infrastructure Handles Requests for a Web Part

While you do not need to understand all the details of how a Web Part is rendered to a page, it is helpful to have a basic understanding of the process. It is important to understand that Web Parts are server controls and can be placed directly in an `.aspx` page. WSS 2.0 and SPS 2003 designate themselves as the default handler for all `.aspx` files. This means that WSS 2.0 and SPS 2003 (not the standard .NET

Framework handler) will receive all requests for pages with the `.aspx` extension. WSS and SPS use a Microsoft SQL Server database to store site content, which includes all data from SharePoint lists, libraries, `.aspx` pages (including all of the WSS/SPS user interface) as well as all the Web Parts contained on `.aspx` pages. The SharePoint ISAPI Filter will process all requests for each port for which it is configured. It is possible to create URLs that will not be processed by the filter by using managed paths. Refer to Chapter 4 for the procedure to exclude paths from SharePoint ISAPI Filter processing.

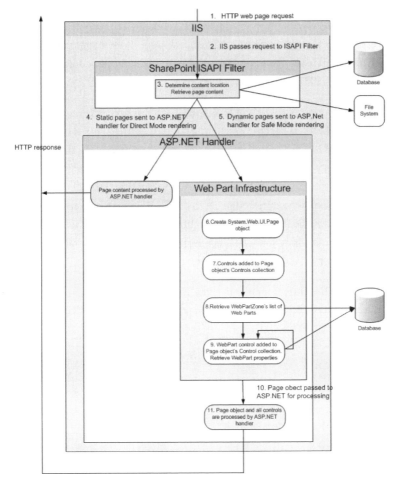

**Figure 3.1:** SharePoint Page Request Workflow.

The page request shown in Figure 3.1 follows these steps:

1.  Microsoft Internet Information Server (IIS) receives a Web Part page request.

2.  IIS passes the request to the SharePoint ISAPI Filter.

3.  The SharePoint ISAPI Filter determines where the content of the page resides and retrieves the content. Site content is either in the database or accessed from a template `.aspx` page. Static pages, such as list management pages, are located on the file system.

4.  If the retrieved page content is static, it is processed by the ASP .NET handler with the resulting output returned as a response to the request. This is called *Direct Mode rendering*. These pages can not be modified using the SharePoint web interface and can contain any legal ASP .NET code or controls.

5.  If the retrieved page content is dynamic (for example, site pages), it is sent to the Web Part infrastructure for processing. This is called *Safe Mode rendering*. All pages that can be modified using the SharePoint web front end are stored in the database. The Web Part infrastructure uses Safe Mode rendering to retrieve the Web Parts that belong on the requested page, to set the Web Part properties, and to determine if the Web Part is allowed to execute on the server. Because Safe Mode rendering is interpreted and not compiled, the use of C# or Visual Basic code within the page itself is not allowed.

6.  The Web Part infrastructure creates an object that derives from the **System.Web.UI.Page** class, which is the base type of a .NET web page.

7.  The Web Part infrastructure parses the retrieved page content and adds any necessary controls to the appropriate control collections:

    -   Server controls in the page content are added as a server controls to the **Page** object's control collection. Controls are verified that they are allowed to execute on the server.

    -   HTML in the page content is added as a **System.Web. UI.WebControls.Literal** object to the **Page** object's control collection.

- **WebPartZone** controls in the page content are added as **Microsoft.SharePoint.WebPartPages.WebPartZone** objects to the **Page** object's control collection.

8. For each **WebPartZone** object added to the **Page** object's control collection, the Web Part infrastructure will retrieve a list of Web Parts associated with the specific **WebPartZone** object from the database. This step is the key to allowing personalization. Dynamic Web Parts and their properties are stored within SQL Server 2000, rather than residing as static controls inside .aspx pages.

9. The Web Part infrastructure will process each Web Part by doing the following:

   - Determining if the Web Part is allowed to execute on the server.

   - Adding an object that derives from the **Microsoft.SharePoint. WebPartPages.WebPart** class to the **Page** object's control collection.

   - Retrieving Web Part properties stored in the database.

   - Applying retrieved Web Part properties to the Web Part control.

10. The Web Part infrastructure passes the **Page** object and the control collection to the ASP .NET handler for rendering. At this point in the process, the page is treated as though it was a basic ASP .NET page from any web application.

11. The ASP .NET handler processes the page. The Web Parts execute and render content as markup, typically as HTML. The controls in the control collection are processed in the order that they were added to the collection, which results in each object rendering its markup to the output. The ASP .NET handler returns the complete page output as a response to the requesting client.

## Web Part Infrastructure Classes

The Web Part infrastructure contains many .NET classes for creating and using Web Parts. The SharePoint Products and Technologies 2003 Software Development Kit is an excellent resource for these classes. It is currently located at `http://msdn.microsoft.com/library/default.asp?url=/library/en-us/spptsdk/html/SPSDKWelcome.asp`. Web Part developers can use these classes and other objects from the Web Part infrastructure in a Web Part. We will use these classes in our examples in this book.

Let's look at a few of the most frequently used Web Part infrastructure classes.

### The Microsoft.SharePoint.WebPartPages.WebPartPage Class

Web pages in WSS and SPS are by default **Microsoft.SharePoint.WebPartPages. WebPartPage** classes. The ISAPI filter will return an error if the requested page does not inherit from the **WebPartPage** class.

The **Microsoft.SharePoint.WebPartPages.WebPartPage** class inherits from the **System.Web.UI.Page** class. Web developers will readily recognize the **Page** class as the standard ASP .NET page object normally processed by the ASP .NET Framework. Each page in WSS and SPS is really a specialized web page. The **WebPartPage** object participates in the ASP .NET Framework like any other standard page and is also responsible for initializing the Web Part infrastructure for Web Part support. The **WebPartPage** object will contain text, code, and controls, as well as Web Part zones, which are container controls for Web Parts.

Visual Studio .NET can be used to create new Web Part pages capable of hosting Web Parts, but that is beyond the scope of this book. The most common way to create a new Web Part page is through the web browser under the **Create** page. The **Create** page is a standard page in WSS and SPS that is used to create new items such as lists, document libraries, and Web Part pages. Figure 3.2 displays the Web Pages section of the **Create** page.

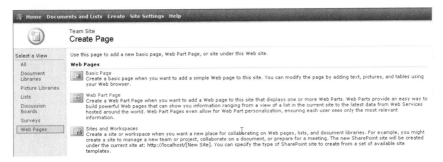

**Figure 3.2:** Creating a New Web Part Page.

## *The Microsoft.SharePoint.WebPartPages.WebPartZone Class*

Web Parts that are added to the page with web browsers are contained in a Web Part zone. The **WebPartZone** class inherits from the **System.Web.UI.Control** class. **WebPartZone** class properties allow the web page designer and developer to control the layout of the zone. Properties of the **WebPartZone** class allow or disallow personalization and customization to the Web Parts contained in the zone. Table 3.1 shows some of the most frequently used properties of the **WebPartZone** class. For a complete list of properties for this class, see the SharePoint Products and Technologies 2003 Software Development Kit.

| PROPERTY | DESCRIPTION |
|---|---|
| AllowCustomization | Allows or disallows users to change properties on the contained Web Parts. Possible values are True or False. |
| AllowPersonalization | Allows or disallows users to store personalized versions of properties of the contained Web Parts. Possible values are True or False. |
| FrameType | Sets the default **FrameType** value for contained Web Parts. This property only affects Web Parts with a **FrameType** of Default. Possible values are: Default, None, Standard or TitleBarOnly. |
| ID | This is a unique identifier for each Web Part zone. This property is inherited from the base **Control** type. |
| Orientation | Determines the layout direction for contained Web Parts. Possible values are Horizontal or Vertical. |
| Title | Friendly name for the Web Part zone. |

**Table 3.1:** Typical Properties of the WebPartZone Class.

## The Microsoft.SharePoint.WebPartPages.WebPart Class

The **Microsoft.SharePoint.WebPartPages.WebPart** class inherits from the **System.Web.UI.Control** class and is therefore a type of web control. The **WebPart** class is of primary interest to Web Part developers because it is the required base class for all custom Web Parts.

Web Parts can contain custom properties decorated with the attribute **WebPartStorage**. Attributes on custom properties are used by the Web Part infrastructure to determine if the property is shared among all users, unique to an individual, or not saved at all. The tool pane is used to display and modify the properties. The **WebPartStorage** attribute is discussed further in Chapter 9.

Web Parts can be placed directly onto a Web Part page (Static) or into a Web Part zone (Dynamic). When placed on a page directly, the Web Part properties are stored in the page and cannot be modified using the web interface.

Table 3.2 displays some of the most frequently used methods of the WebPart class. For a complete list of methods for this class, see the *SharePoint Products and Technologies 2003 Software Development Kit.*

| METHOD | DESCRIPTION |
|---|---|
| CanRunAt | Used to determine where a connection interface is allowed to run. Returns a **ConnectionRunAt** enumeration value. |
| CreateWebPartMenu | Override this virtual method to create a custom Web Part menu. |
| EnsureInterfaces | Used with Web Parts that implement a connection interface. This method is called when the Web Part is expected to register its interfaces with the Web Part infrastructure. |
| GetData | Called during the PreRender event to allow a Web Part to retrieve data. |
| GetToolParts | Override this virtual function when using custom tool parts in the tool pane. |
| OnDataBinding | Virtual method that can be overridden. Called when the Web Part page is binding a control to a data source. |
| OnInit | Virtual method that can be overridden. Called when the Web Part is being initialized. |
| OnLoad | Virtual method that can be overridden. Called when the Web Part is loading. |
| OnPreRender | Virtual method that can be overridden. Called just prior to Web Part rendering. |
| OnUnload | Virtual method that can be overridden. Called when the Web Part is unloading. |
| PartCommunicationConnect | Method called by the Web Part infrastructure to notify a connected Web Part to send data to the connected Web Parts. |
| PartCommunicationInit | Method called by the Web Part infrastructure to notify the Web Part to initialize its connectable interfaces. |
| PartCommunicationMain | Method called by the Web Part infrastructure to notify a connected Web Part to send data to the connected Web Parts. |
| RegisterInterface | Method that registers the Web Part's connectable interfaces with the Web Part infrastructure. |
| Render | An inherited method from the base **Control** type. Web Parts should not utilize this method. |
| RenderWebPart | Method that renders the Web Part content to the output buffer. |
| ReplaceToken | Replaces tokens in a string, often used to make HTML output unique. |

**Table 3.2:** Methods of the WebPart Class.

Table 3.3 shows some of the more frequently used properties of the **WebPart** class. For a complete list of properties for this class, see the SharePoint Products and Technologies 2003 Software Development Kit.

| PROPERTY | DESCRIPTION |
|---|---|
| AllowMinimize | Determines if a user can minimize the Web Part. |
| AllowRemove | Determines if a user can remove the Web Part. |
| AllowZoneChange | Determines if a user can move the Web Part to a different zone. |
| Connections | Stores information about how a connection is made between connectable Web Parts. |
| Description | Returns or sets the value used when hovering over the title of the Web Part, either on the page or in the gallery. |
| DetailLink | Links to a page with details or more information. |
| EffectiveStorage | Determines if the Web Part properties have been personalized or are still shared. |
| EffectiveTitle | Returns the actual runtime title, which may have been modified to ensure a unique title. |
| FrameState | Returns or sets the **FrameState** property, which can be `Normal` or `Minimized`. |
| FrameStyle | The style of the frame. Can be `Default`, `None`, `Standard`, or `TitleBarOnly`. If `Default`, it will use the WebPartZone's **FrameType** property value. |
| Height | The height of the Web Part, expressed in measurements supported by HTML or CSS. |
| HelpLink | Returns or sets a link and displays the **Help** menu items for the Web Part menu. |
| IsIncluded | Determines if a Web Part is included on the page. If this is set to false, the Web Part is available in the Web Part Page Gallery. |
| IsVisible | Determines if the Web Part content is visible. If this property is false, the Web Part will still render but the content will not be visible. |
| MissingAssembly | Returns or sets the message that will be displayed if the assembly is not available on the server. |
| PartOrder | The order of the Web Part within the Web Part zone. |
| Qualifier | The unique ID for the Web Part on the page. Suitable for inclusion in JavaScript names for use in generating client-side scripts. |
| SaveProperties | Returns or sets the flag that determines if the properties have changed on the Web Part. |
| Title | Returns or sets the title that is displayed in the Title Bar. |
| Width | The fixed width of the Web Part, expressed in measurements supported by HTML or CSS. |
| ZoneID | Returns or sets the Zone ID for the Web Part. |

**Table 3.3:** Typical Properties of the WebPart Class.

# Part II

# Creating Basic Web Parts

RATIONAL
PRESS

# Chapter 4

# Using the Web Control Library Template

This chapter provides an extended example of creating a basic Web Part with the **Web Control Library** template and importing its definition file into a Windows SharePoint Services (WSS) or Microsoft SharePoint Portal Server (SPS) site. The **Web Control Library** template is a Visual Studio .NET template that installs with Visual Studio .NET. The example in this chapter is shown in WSS, but the procedures will work equally well for both SPS and WSS sites.

> *Note:*
>
> The example in this chapter is in Visual C#. The example uses Visual Studio .NET and Visual C# and requires you to have Visual Studio .NET and WSS running on the same machine.

## Creating the Development Environment

To start creating Web Parts, you will need to set up your development environment, which should include all necessary hardware and software to develop Web Parts. A development environment must include access to either WSS 2.0 or SPS 2003, as well as development tools. Most of the examples in this book will only need WSS, but some of the examples will require SPS to access resources specific to SPS. It is beyond the scope of this book to discuss the installation options for these products; see your WSS or SPS installation documentation for details. Refer to Chapter 1 for the current minimal hardware requirements for a development environment.

In the examples in this book, Visual Studio .NET will be used to develop Web Parts. During the Visual Studio .NET installation, be sure to select your preferred language or languages. Web Parts can be developed in any .NET language, such as Visual C# or Visual Basic .NET. The development environment should also have the latest version of Microsoft Internet Explorer and the latest software security updates.

There are two possible ways to develop Web Parts with Visual Studio .NET: locally or remotely. Developers can either log on to the server locally or use remote access to log on to the server. The best scenario for Web Part development with Visual Studio .NET is to install Visual Studio .NET on the development environment's WSS or SPS server. Developing on the server will allow a developer to develop more efficiently and effectively. To develop on the WSS or SPS server, simply install Visual Studio .NET on the server. All examples of Web Parts in this book have been developed locally on the SharePoint server.

Many companies do not allow developers to work locally on a server box. It is possible to develop remotely on a workstation, but this option is not as efficient as developing locally on the server. To work remotely from a workstation, you must have Visual Studio .NET installed on the workstation. The `Microsoft.SharePoint.dll` file must be copied locally from the SharePoint server and referenced from the Visual Studio .NET project. The Microsoft.SharePoint.dll file resides at `<root>\Program Files\Common Files\Microsoft Shared\web server extensions\60\ISAPI\` in a default installation. Web Parts can be created locally and the resulting Web Part assembly can then be moved to the virtual server's `bin` directory on the SharePoint server.

## *Managing Paths in WSS and SPS*

Many developers attempt to develop other non-Web Part applications on the development server, including web applications. WSS and SPS install an ISAPI filter that looks at all incoming HTTP requests and can perform processing on those requests. This filter will attempt to handle all ASPX requests and treat them as though they are part of the WSS and SPS server. If you attempt to create a web application or Web Services on the same virtual server as WSS or SPS, the paths to the web application or Web Services project files will not be available, because all paths are considered to be managed by WSS and SPS.

Allowing web application development is as simple as marking a path as excluded, so that WSS and SPS will not attempt process it. The request will instead be processed by the standard ASP .NET handler. To mark a path as excluded, you must configure a managed path of type **Excluded**.

Use the following procedure to configure an excluded path in WSS or SPS:

1.  Use the command line to navigate to:

    ```
    <root>\Program Files\Common Files\Microsoft Shared\web
    server extensions\60\bin\.
    ```

2.  Use the following syntax to run stsadm.exe using the **addpath** operation.

    **SYNTAX**

    ```
    Stsadm -o addpath -url <excluded site url> -type exclusion
    ```

    **EXAMPLE**

    ```
    Stsadm -o addpath -url  http://WSS1/NonWSSApps  -type exclusion
    ```

# Creating and Deploying a Web Part

There are four steps to create and deploy a Web Part on a Web Part page:

1. **Create the Web Part** — Use Visual Studio .NET to create an assembly containing the Web Part.

2. **Create the Web Part definition file** — This is the .dwp file that describes the Web Part, its assembly, and class.

3. **Mark the Web Part safe to render** — Modify the web.config file to mark the assembly and the class or classes as safe to render.

4. **Deploy the Web Part** — Import the Web Part definition file and add the Web Part to a Web Part zone in a Web Part page.

## Creating the Web Part

Let's begin by creating a simple Web Part based on the **Microsoft.SharePoint. WebPartPages.WebPart** class. This Web Part, called **Hello Rational Press**, will display a greeting to the end user. It will contain a single text property named **Greeting** that will hold the value to be displayed. Figure 4.1 shows the finished **Hello Rational Press** Web Part.

**Figure 4.1:** Hello Rational Press Web Part.

There are three procedures necessary to create the Web Part:

▶  Create the Web Part project.

▶  Create a custom property.

▶  Override the **RenderWebPart** method.

### Create the Web Part Project

1.  In Visual Studio .NET, select **New Project** and choose the **Web Control Library** template. Figure 4.2 shows the **New Project** dialog box and the **Web Control Library** template.

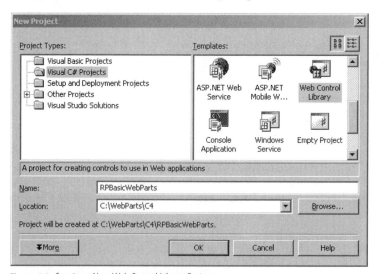

**Figure 4.2:** Creating a New Web Control Library Project.

2. Provide a name in the **Name** field for the **Web Control Library** project. In our example, the **Web Control Library** project is named **RPBasicWebParts**.

> *Tech Tip:*
>
> **The project name you select will be the default value for the namespace and the assembly. You can change it later, but it is simpler if you think of a meaningful name now. The fully qualified name, which is the combination of the namespace and class name, will be used in various locations.**

3. Click the **OK** button to create the new **Web Control Library** project. Figure 4.3 displays the files created for the new project.

**Figure 4.3:** Project Files for the RPBasicWebParts Project.

4. Give the `WebCustomControl1.cs` file a more useful name by right-clicking the file in the Visual Studio .NET **Solution Explorer** pane and selecting the **Rename** menu item. Each code file can contain multiple Web Part classes. Renaming the code file is not required, but using the default name of `WebCustomControl1.cs` can lead to confusion. For this example, we'll change the name of the `WebCustomControl1.cs` file to `wpRationalPressBasic.cs`.

5. Add a `System.xml.dll` reference to the project. Because Web Part properties are serialized as XML, this reference is required. To reference the `System.xml.dll`, right-click the **References** folder in the Visual Studio .NET **Solution Explorer** pane. Select **Add a Reference** from the pop-up menu and choose **System.xml.dll** from the list on the **.NET** tab. Click the **Select** button to add the `System.xml.dll` file to the list of selected components. Click the **OK** button to exit the **Add Reference** dialog box.

6. Add a reference to the `Microsoft.SharePoint.dll` file. This assembly contains many of the Web Part infrastructure classes. To add the reference, right-click the **References** folder in the Visual Studio .NET **Solution Explorer** pane. Select **Add a Reference** from the pop-up menu. Click **Browse** and navigate to the `Microsoft.SharePoint.dll` file. The default location for the assembly is `<root>\Program Files\Common Files\Microsoft Shared\Web Server Extensions\60\ISAPI\Microsoft.Sharepoint. dll`. Select **Microsoft.Sharepoint.dll** and click the **Open** button to add it to the list of selected components. Click the **OK** button to exit the **Add Reference** dialog box. Figure 4.4 displays the **References** folder in the Visual Studio .NET **Solution Explorer** pane.

**Figure 4.4:** Solution Explorer Pane Displaying Project References.

7.  In the `wpRationalPressBasic.cs` file (named `WebCustomControl1.cs` by default), use the following syntax to add **using** statements, so that you will not have to fully qualify object names for objects belonging to the **Microsoft.SharePoint.WebPartPages** and **System.Xml.Serialization** namespaces.

**SYNTAX**

```
using <Namespace>;
```

**EXAMPLE**

```
using Microsoft.SharePoint.WebPartPages;
using System.Xml.Serialization;
```

8.  In the `wpRationalPressBasic.cs`. file (named `WebCustomControl1.cs` by default), change the default namespace from **WebControlLibrary** class to a more descriptive namespace. The namespace will help uniquely identify the project's classes and methods.

**SYNTAX**

```
namespace <namespace value>
```

**EXAMPLE**

```
namespace RPBasicWebParts
```

9.  Change the base class of the **WebCustomControl1** class from **System.Web.UI.WebControls.WebControl** to **Microsoft. SharePoint.WebPartPages.WebPart**, located in the `wpRationalPressBasic.cs`. file (named `WebCustomControl1.cs` by default).

SYNTAX

```
<scope> class <class name> : <base type>
```

EXAMPLE

```
public class WebCustomControl1  : Microsoft.SharePoint.
WebPartPages.WebPart
```

10. In the wpRationalPressBasic.cs file (named WebCustomControl1.
cs by default), rename the **WebCustomControl1** class. For this
example, change the name to HelloRationalPress, like this:

```
public class HelloRationalPress: Microsoft.SharePoint.
WebPartPages.WebPart
```

11. Add the **XmlRoot** attribute to the **WebPart** class. Custom
properties are serialized to XML with a root namespace provided
by the **XmlRoot** attribute.

SYNTAX

```
XmlRoot(Namespace="<namespace here>")
```

EXAMPLE

```
XmlRoot(Namespace="RationalPressWebParts")
```

12. Configure your project's **Output Path** property to point to the
bin directory of the virtual server. The assembly that results from
building the project must reside in the bin directory of the virtual
server, or in the *Global Assembly Cache* (GAC). In our example,
the **RPBasicWebParts** project will build the assembly and place it
in the virtual server's bin directory. In Visual Studio .NET, choose
**Project ⇨ <your project name> Properties** to open your project's
**Property Pages** dialog box. For the **RPBasicWebParts** project,
choose **RPBasicWebParts Properties**. The project's **Property
Pages** dialog box will appear.

13. From the left-hand pane of the **Property Pages** dialog box, select **Configuration Properties** ⇨ **Build**. The **Output Path** value is listed under the **Outputs** section. Browse to the site's `bin` directory and click the **Open** button to choose the directory. Click the **OK** button to exit the project's **Property Pages** dialog box.

Figure 4.5 shows the **Property Pages** dialog box with the **Output Path** value set to the virtual server's `bin` directory.

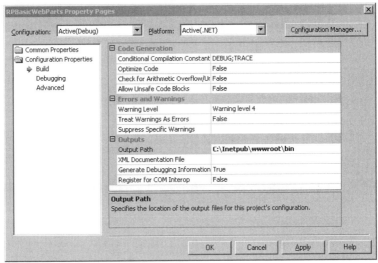

**Figure 4.5:** Property Pages Dialog Box for the Project.

> ### *Note:*
> A site's `bin` **directory is usually located at** <root>\inetpub\wwwroot\bin. **The location of the** `bin` **directory depends on the virtual root's IIS settings. If the** `bin` **directory does not exist at the virtual server root level, you must create a new folder named** `bin`.

## Create a Custom Property

Web Parts expose custom properties that enable you to configure and modify content. You can modify custom properties by using the tool pane in design mode, as described in Chapter 2.

To create a custom property, follow these steps:

1. Use the following syntax to create a new property in the **WebPart** class.

**SYNTAX**

```
public <variable type> <Property Name>
{
        get
        {
                return <property value>;
        }
        set
        {
                <Property Name> = value;
        }
}
```

**EXAMPLE**

```
public string Greeting
{
        get
        {
                return greeting;
        }
        set
        {
                greeting = value;
        }
}
```

This example creates the **Greeting** property for the **HelloRationalPress WebPart** class.

2.  Use the following syntax to add attributes to the new property:

**SYNTAX**

```
[Browsable(<true|false>),
Category(<category name>),
DefaultValue(<default value>),
WebPartStorage(<Strorage.Shared|Storage.Personal|Storage.None>),
FriendlyName(<string value for display name>),
Description(<string value for ToolTips>)]
```

**EXAMPLE**

```
[Browsable(true),
Category("Miscellaneous"),
DefaultValue(Default _ Greeting),
WebPartStorage(Storage.Shared),
FriendlyName("Greeting Message"),
Description("The Greeting to be displayed")]
```

The following attributes provide the following additional information about a given object:

- **Browsable (true/false)** — Determines if the property is visible within the tool pane.

- **Category (string value)** — Denotes the section of the tool pane in which the property will be displayed. If the section does not exist, it will be created.

- **DefaultValue (various types of values)** — The starting value of the property.

- **WebPartStorage (Personal/Shared/None)** — Determines if the property is persistent and if it is available on a per-user basis or shared with all users.

- **FriendlyName (string)** — The name that will be shown in the tool pane. This will override the property name.

- **Description** — The text to be displayed as a ToolTip.

3. The **DefaultValue** attribute requires a constant value rather than a variable. You must also create a class-level variable to store the property's content. Use the following syntax to add the default constant and a variable to hold the content of the property.

**SYNTAX**

```
<scope> const <type> <constant name> = value;
<scope><type><variable name> = value;
```

**EXAMPLE**

```
private const string Default_ Greeting =
"Hello Rational Press!";
private string greeting = Default_ Greeting ;
```

Listing 4.1 displays the **Default_Greeting** constant and the string variable named **greeting** for the **Hello Rational Press** Web Part.

```
private const string Default_ Greeting =
"Hello Rational Press!";
private string greeting = Default_ Greeting ;


[Browsable(true),Category("Miscellaneous"),
DefaultValue(Default_ Greeting),
WebPartStorage(Storage.Shared),
FriendlyName("Greeting Message"),
Description("The Greeting to be displayed")]
public string Greeting
{
        get
        {
                return greeting;
        }
        set
        {
                greeting = value;
```

```
        }
    }
```

**Listing 4.1:** The Greeting Property.

## *Override the RenderWebPart Method*

To render the Web Part, the **RenderWebPart** method of the **WebPart** class must be overridden. The **RenderWebPart** method creates the HTML that describes the Web Part to the browser. Because the project was originally a **Web Control Library** project, the included class (named **WebCustomControl1** by default) contains an overridden **Render** method. In a web control, this function is called when the control needs to render its markup to the output stream. The **WebPart** class contains a **RenderWebPart** method which should be used to replace the **Render** function.

### Caution:

**A Web Part should never define a Render method. Instead, it should define a RenderWebPart method. The Render method will not create the required base markup for the Web Part.**

To override the **WebPart** class's **RenderWebPart** method:

1. In Visual Studio .NET, delete the **Render** method from the **WebPart** class. For this example, remove the **Render** method from the **HelloRationalPress** class.

2. Use the following syntax to add the **RenderWebPart** method to the Web Part class:

```
protected override void
RenderWebPart(HtmlTextWriter output)
{
}
```

3. Use the methods available to the **HtmlTextWriter** class to send HTML to the output buffer, which will send it on to the client. For example, Listing 4.2 uses the **Write** method to send the value of the **greeting** variable to the output buffer. The **HtmlEncode** method is used to ensure that no special HTML characters are placed in the output buffer. For more information on methods available to the **HtmlTextWriter** class, as well as the SPEncode's **HtmlEncode** method, see Chapter 8.

```
protected override void RenderWebPart(HtmlTextWriter
output)
{
        output.Write(Microsoft.SharePoint.Utilities.SPEncode.
⮑ HtmlEncode(greeting));
}
```

**Listing 4.2:** The HelloRationalPress Web Part's RenderWebPart Method.

4. Save the project.

5. Build the **Web Part Control Library** project in the virtual server's `bin` directory by selecting **Build** ⇨ **Build Solution** from the Visual Studio .NET menu. The project will be checked for errors. If no errors are present, building the project will result in an assembly stored at the location of the **Output Path** property.

## Creating the Web Part Definition File

The Web Part definition file (`.dwp`) details Web Part properties, as well as the location of the Web Part's assembly and its class name. Use the following procedure to add the Web Part definition file to the Web Control Project.

1. Add a new XML file by right-clicking the project name in the Visual Studio .NET **Solution Explorer** pane and choose **Add New Item** ⇨ **XML File**. Provide a name that has a file extension of `.dwp` and click the **Open** button. Our example adds a new XML file named `HelloRationalPress.dwp`.

2.  Modify the Web Part definition file's XML. Because the XML in the definition file is specific to each Web Part instance, you must modify the definition file to match the Web Part.

**SYNTAX**

```
<?xml version="1.0"?>
<WebPart
        xmlns="http://schemas.microsoft.com/WebPart/v2">
        <Assembly>
                <!--Assembly Name without the extension-->
        </Assembly>
        <TypeName>
                <!--Namespace and class name-->
        </TypeName>
        <Title>
                <!--Title to appear in titlebar-->
        </Title>
        <Description>
                <!--Text that will display in tool tips-->
        </Description>
</WebPart>
```

**EXAMPLE**

```
<?xml version="1.0"?>
<WebPart
        xmlns="http://schemas.microsoft.com/WebPart/v2">
        <Assembly>RPBasicWebParts</Assembly>
        <TypeName>RPBasicWebParts.HelloRationalPress
        ➲ </TypeName>
        <Title>Hello Rational Press</Title>
        <Description>A simple Web Part using C#</Description>
</WebPart>
```

> **Note:**
>
> The definition file is written in XML and is case sensitive. The file will not parse correctly if there is a space at the beginning of the file.

3. Save the modified definition file.

> **Note:**
>
> When deploying the Web Part assembly to the `bin` directory, the **Assembly** element requires the name of the assembly. When deploying the Web Part assembly to the Global Assembly Cache, the **Assembly** element requires the assembly name, version, culture and public key information. For more information on deploying an assembly to the Global Assembly Cache, see Chapter 11.

## Marking the Web Part Safe to Render

For a Web Part to run, it must be listed in the **SafeControls** section of the `web.config` file as safe to render. The `web.config` file contains configuration information for the virtual directory and associated web applications. The **SafeControl** elements in the **SafeControls** section of the `web.config` file allow server administrators to control which Web Parts are allowed to run on the server. Requiring Web Parts to be marked as safe to render also allows administrators to disable specific Web Parts, including those that are installed by WSS or SPS.

> **Caution:**
>
> Importing a definition file only imports a particular definition or configuration of a Web Part. It does not install the required assembly, nor does it mark the Web Part as safe to render.

To add a **SafeControl** entry in the **SafeControls** section of the web.config file:

1.  Open the web.config file in Notepad. You will need to navigate
    to the virtual server's root directory (usually <root>\inetpub\
    wwwroot) to locate the web.config file. When looking for the web.
    config file, be sure that the **Open** dialog box has a **Files of types**
    value of All Files.

2.  Choose **Edit** ➪ **Find** to find the **SafeControls** element. Enter
    <SafeControls> in the text box, then click the **Find Next** button.

3.  Use the following syntax to add a new **SafeControl** element inside
    the **SafeControls** element.

**SYNTAX**

```
<SafeControl Assembly="<!-Assembly name"
        Namespace="Namespace"
        TypeName="Specific class name or*"
        Safe="True|False"/>
```

**EXAMPLE**

```
<SafeControl Assembly="RPBasicWebParts"
        Namespace="RPBasicWebParts"
        TypeName="*"
        Safe="True"/>
```

*Note:*

**If a Web Part fails to render on a page, it is usually due to an incorrect
SafeControl entry.**

4.  Save the web.config file.

Web Parts can be marked *unsafe* for rendering by changing the **Safe** attribute to
False. The **Safe** attribute is set to True by default.

*Tech Tip:*

To mark a Web Part in the GAC as safe for rendering, the **Assembly** attribute will require assembly name, version, culture, and public key information. **Chapter 11** will show how to create a public key and install the assembly into the GAC.

## Deploying the Web Part

Once the Web Part has been built, the definition modified, and the Web Part marked in the `web.config` file as safe to render, the Web Part definition can be added to a page by importing its definition file.

To import a Web Part definition file:

1.  From the **Modify Shared Page** link in the upper-right corner of the page, choose **Add Web Parts ⇨ Import**. The tool pane will be displayed at the right-hand side of the web browser.

2.  Click the **Browse** button and use the **Choose File** dialog box to navigate to the definition file (`.dwp`). For this example, navigate to the `HelloRationalPress.dwp` file.

3.  Click the **Upload** button. The definition file is uploaded to the server and the tool pane lists the Web Part. Figure 4.6 shows the **Hello Rational Press** Web Part in the tool pane.

**Figure 4.6:** Custom Web Part Imported in the Tool Pane.

4. Drag the icon next to the Web Part to a Web Part zone on the page. If the Web Part does not open in a Web Part zone, check the tool pane for any error messages. Figure 4.7 shows a common error message that occurs after attempting to drop the Web Part into a zone.

**Figure 4.7:** Error Message When Attempting to Display a Control Not Marked As Safe.

> **Note:**
>
> If adding a Web Part to a Web Part zone creates an error, the most likely causes will be incorrect `web.config` file entries or incorrect definition (`.dwp`) files. Look carefully at both the SafeControl entry and the definition file to find the error. Common mistakes are misspellings, an incorrect namespace, or incorrect assembly information.

5. Close the tool pane.

Once the Web Part renders its content to a page successfully, try modifying the custom property and displaying different text messages.

**Bonus:**

You can download the code in this chapter (in both Visual C# and Visual Basic .NET) free of charge, if you register this book at www.rationalpress.com.

# Chapter 5

# Using the Visual Studio .NET Web Part Templates

This chapter shows you how to create Web Parts from the Visual Studio .NET Web Part templates. Chapter 4 demonstrated how to create a simple Web Part, starting with the **Web Control Library** template. The Visual Studio .NET Web Part templates provide a better starting point for creating Web Parts because they add code and definition files that are specific to Web Parts. The Visual Studio .NET Web Part templates create a new Visual Studio .NET project, complete with the files, references, import statements, and common code that a Web Part requires. The templates create a definition file and will even populate some of the fields, saving keystrokes and preventing spelling errors.

This chapter shows how to install the Web Part templates for Visual Studio .NET and create a basic Web Part using the **Web Part Library** project template. The example in this chapter is shown in Windows SharePoint Services (WSS), but the procedures will work equally well for both WSS and Microsoft SharePoint Portal Server (SPS) sites.

## *Web Part Templates for Visual Studio .NET*

Web Part Templates for Microsoft Visual Studio .NET Web Parts are free additions to the Visual Studio .NET development environment. Download the installation file and use the provided templates to create new Web Parts. You can install templates for both Visual C# and Visual Basic .NET. The templates installed with the download include:

▶ **Web Part Library** — This project template is used to start a new Web Part project.

▶ **Consumer Web Part** — This file template provides the basic code for a connected Web Part that consumes information from a Provider Web Part. (A connected Web Part can connect to other Web Parts and exchange information.)

▶ **Provider Web Part** — This file template provides the basic code for a connected Web Part that provides information to a Consumer Web Part.

▶ **Tool Part** — This file template provides the basic code to start a **ToolPart** class. A tool part object is used to display Web Part properties in the tool pane.

▶ **Web Part** — This file template provides the basic code to start a Web Part. It includes a **WebPart** class.

▶ **Web Part Definition File** — This template provides the basic XML to describe a specific instance of a Web Part.

▶ **WPManifest** — This template provides the starting point for describing Web Parts to an installation program. For more information on the `Manifest.xml` file, see Chapter 11.

## *Installing the Web Part Templates for Visual Studio .NET*

Before using the Visual Studio .NET Web Part templates, you must download and install them on the development machine.

To download and install the Visual Studio .NET Web Part templates:

1. Download the file **Web Part Templates for Microsoft Visual Studio .NET** from Microsoft. This installation file is located at: `http://www.microsoft.com/downloads/details.aspx?FamilyId=CAC3E0D2-BEC1-494C-A74E-75936B88E3B5&displaylang=en`. If this link fails, search for `Web Part Template` on Microsoft's MSDN site at `http://www.msdn.microsoft.com/`.

2. Double-click the installation file to unpack it. This will uncompress the files into a local folder. Select a folder and remember where the extracted files are sent.

3.  Run `Setup.Exe` from the extracted file location.

4.  From the **Web Part Templates for Microsoft Visual Studio .NET Setup Wizard**, click the **Next** button, agree to the license requirements, and select which templates to install (Visual Basic .NET, Visual C#, or both). Click the **Next** button.

5.  Use the wizard to browse to the location where you want to install the templates.

6.  Click the **Next** button to begin installation. The selected templates will be installed at the specified location.

7.  Close the wizard.

# Creating and Deploying Web Parts with the Web Part Library Template

Creating a Web Part with the **Web Part Library** project template requires you to follow similar steps to those discussed in Chapter 4. While a template will help you complete the basic steps for creating and deploying a Web Part, you must nonetheless ensure that all the steps are completed.

1.  **Create the Web Part** — Use Visual Studio .NET to create an assembly containing the Web Part.

2.  **Modify the Web Part definition file** — This is the `.dwp` file that describes the Web Part, its assembly and its class. The **Web Part Library** template will create the definition file for you, but you will need to modify it.

3.  **Mark the Web Part safe to render** — Modify the `web.config` file to mark the assembly and the class or classes as safe to render.

4.  **Deploy the Web Part** — Import the Web Part definition file and add the Web Part to a Web Part zone in a Web Part page.

This chapter shows how to use the Visual Studio .NET **Web Part Library** project template to create and deploy a Web Part called **Site Navigator**. This is a simple Web Part that will create links to subsites of the current site and allow end users to access them. The **Site Navigator** Web Part provides a simple visual clue to the end user that accessible subsites exist, and provides links to those subsites. **Site Navigator** will access the sites using the WSS Object Model, which is how you programmatically access the data and functionality of WSS. The **Site Navigator** Web Part includes a single custom property called **Show_Events**. When a user sets the **Show_Events** value to `true` in the tool pane, the Web Part will display basic trace information within the Web Part frame. Figure 5.1 shows the **Site Navigator** Web Part.

**Site Navigator** ▼
Ben's Cement Company Project
Betsy's Equine Center SPS Project
Darrins Health System WSS Project
Meg's Horse Farm Project
SharePoint Tech Research Center

**Figure 5.1:** Site Navigator Web Part.

*Caution:*

**Before creating Web Parts, be sure your development environment is set up correctly. For details on creating a development environment, see Chapter 4.**

## Creating the Web Part

Creating the **Site Navigator** Web Part with the **Web Part Library** project template requires you to complete the following steps. Two of the steps are generally optional, but are necessary for the **Site Navigator** example.

▶ Create the Web Part project.

▶ Create a custom property.

▶ Add WSS Object Model code. (Required for our example)

▶ Create the trace message. (Required for our example)

▶ Modify the **RenderWebPart** method.

## Create the Web Part Project

Use the following procedure to create the Web Part project:

1.  Open Visual Studio .NET, click the **New Project** button, and choose the **Web Part Library** template. Figure 5.2 shows the **New Project** dialog box with the **Web Part Library** template.

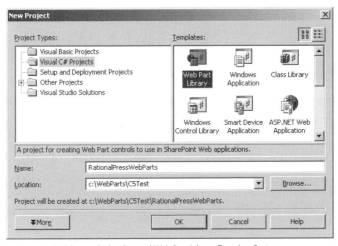

**Figure 5.2:** New Project Dialog Box and Web Part Library Template Project.

2.  Provide a name in the **Name** field for the Web Part project. The example Web Part project is named **RationalPressWebParts**.

3.  Click the **OK** button to create the new **Web Part Library** project. Figure 5.3 shows the files created for the new project.

**Figure 5.3:** Files and References Created in a Web Part Library Project.

4. Give the `WebPart1.cs` file a more descriptive name by right-clicking the file in the Visual Studio .NET **Solution Explorer** pane and selecting the **Rename** menu item. Each code file can contain multiple **WebPart** classes. Renaming the code file is not required, but using the default name of `WebPart1.cs` can lead to confusion. For this example, we'll change the name of the `WebPart1.cs` file to `WebParts.cs`.

5. In the `WebParts.cs` file (named `WebPart1.cs` by default), rename the **WebPart1** class. For this example, we'll change the name of the **WebPart1** class to **SiteNavigator**.

6. Change the namespace in the declaration in `WebParts.cs` from **WebPartLibrary1** to a more useful name. The namespace fully qualifies and identifies the Web Part, and defaults to the project name. The namespace of the **Site Navigator** Web Part is **RationalPress.WebParts**.

7. Configure your project's **Output Path** property to point to the `bin` directory of the virtual server, as described in Chapter 4. In our example, the **Site Navigator** Web Part project will build the Web Part assembly and place it in the virtual server's `bin` directory. In Visual Studio .NET, choose **Project ⇨ <your project name> Properties** to open your project's **Property Pages** dialog box. For the **RationalPressWebParts** project, choose **RationalPressWebParts Properties**. The project's **Property Pages** dialog box will appear.

8. From the left-hand pane of the **Property Pages** dialog box, select **Configuration Properties ⇨ Build**. The **Output Path** value is listed under the **Outputs** section. Browse to the site's `bin` directory and click the **Open** button to choose the directory. Click the **OK** button to exit the project's **Property Pages** dialog box.

## Create a Custom Property

Web Parts expose custom properties that enable users to configure and modify content. You can modify custom properties by using the tool pane in design mode, as described in Chapter 2.

To create a custom property in the **WebPart** class:

1. Use the following syntax to create a new property in the **WebPart** class:

**SYNTAX**

```
public <variable type> <Property Name>
{
        get
        {
                return <property value>;
        }
        set
        {
                <Property Name> = value;
        }
}
```

**EXAMPLE**

```
public bool Show _ Events
{
        get
        {
                return ShowEvents;
        }
        set
        {
                ShowEvents = value;
        }
}
```

The example creates the **Show_Events** property for the **SiteNavigator WebPart** class. This example allows the **Show_ Events** property to appear in the tool pane, where users can set it to a value of `true` to display trace information in the Web Part.

2.  Use the following syntax to add attributes to the property:

**SYNTAX**

```
[Browsable(<true|false>),
Category(<category name>),
DefaultValue(<default value>),
WebPartStorage(<Strorage.Shared|
        Storage.Personal|Storage.None>),
FriendlyName(<string value for display name>),
Description(<string value for ToolTips>)]
```

**EXAMPLE**

```
[Browsable(true),
Category("Miscellaneous"),
DefaultValue(defaultShowEvents),
WebPartStorage(Storage.Shared),
FriendlyName("Show Events"),
Description("Show Web Part Events")]
```

These attributes provide the following additional information about a given object:

- **Browsable (true/false)** — Determines if the property is visible within the tool pane.

- **Category (string value)** — Denotes the section of the tool pane in which the property will be displayed. If the section does not exist, it will be created.

- **DefaultValue (various types of values)** — The starting value of the property.

- **WebPartStorage (Personal/Shared/None)**— Determines if the property is persistent and if it is available on a per-user basis or shared with all users.

- **FriendlyName (string)** — The name that will be shown in the tool pane. This will override the property name.

- **Description** — The text to be displayed as a ToolTip.

3. The **DefaultValue** attribute requires a constant value that is defined in the **WebPart** class. You must also create a class-level variable to store the property's content. Use the following syntax to add the default constant and a variable to hold the content of the property.

**SYNTAX**

```
<scope> const <type> <constant name> = value;
<scope><type><variable name> = value;
```

**EXAMPLE**

```
private const bool defaultShowEvents = false;
private bool ShowEvents = defaultShowEvents;
```

Listing 5.1 displays the **defaultShowEvents** constant and the **ShowEvents** variable for the **Site Navigator** Web Part.

```
private const bool defaultShowEvents = false;
private bool ShowEvents = defaultShowEvents;

[Browsable(true),
Category("Miscellaneous"),
DefaultValue(defaultShowEvents ),
WebPartStorage(Storage.Shared),
FriendlyName("Show Events"),
Description("Show Web Part Events")]
public bool Show _ Events
{
        get
        {
                return ShowEvents;
        }
        set
        {
                ShowEvents = value;
        }
}
```

**Listing 5.1:** Show_Events Property.

> ## Tech Tip:
> The default code for the **WebPart** class contains a custom property called **Text**. If this property is not needed, as in the **Site Navigator** Web Part, it can be deleted, or modified to a property that is needed.

## Add WSS Object Model Code

The **Site Navigator** Web Part in our example uses WSS Object Model code to determine the list of subsites available to the users. Listing 5.2 shows how to add the **GetSiteList** method to the **SiteNavigator** class to determine which subsites are available. The **GetSiteList** method calls the WSS **GetContextWeb** method of the WSS object model to return an **SPWeb** object. For this **SPWeb** object, the **GetSubwebsForCurrentUser** method is called to return a collection of individual subwebs for the web site, including the **Title**, **URL**, and **Description** properties of each subweb. The code iterates through each item in the collection and builds a string array that is returned to the calling statement. The code displayed in Listing 5.2 is specific to the **Site Navigator** example; it is not needed for every Web Part.

```
private string[,] GetSiteList()
{
        string[,] webInfo;
        int counter = 0;

        SPWeb web =
                Microsoft.SharePoint.WebControls.SPControl.
                        GetContextWeb(Context);
        SPWebCollection webs =  web.GetSubwebsForCurrentUser( );
        webInfo = new string [webs.Count,3];
        foreach (SPWeb w in webs)
        {
                webInfo[counter,0] = w.Title;
                webInfo[counter,1] = w.Url;
                webInfo[counter++,2] =w.Description;
        }
```

```
        return webInfo;
}
```

**Listing 5.2:** GetSiteList Method That Accesses WSS Object Model.

Although this code is very simple, it will not run under the default WSS and SPS security settings, which do not allow WSS Object Model access from a Web Part. Use the following procedure to set access security to allow our Web Part to access the WSS object model:

1.  Open the `web.config` file in Notepad. Using Notepad, navigate to the virtual server's root directory. The root directory is usually <root>\ `inetpub\wwwroot`. Select the `web.config` file, which contains configuration information for the virtual directory and associated web applications.

2.  Find the **trust** element by clicking **Edit** ⇨ **Find**. Type WSS _ `Minimal`, and click the **Find Next** button.

3.  Set the **trust** element's **level** attribute to **WSS_Medium.** The **WSS_Medium** trust level will allow the Web Part to access the WSS object model. The **trust** element should look like this:

    ```
    <trust level="WSS _ Medium" originUrl="" />
    ```

4.  Save the `web.config` file.

See Chapter 6 for more detailed information on security settings.

## Create the Trace Message

Our example Web Part will display a simple trace message that shows how the code progresses during execution. (For more information on trace messages, see Chapter 7.) We must create this trace message before outputting any HTML. The code to create the message is shown in Listing 5.3. This code will add its part of the message to the **Message** variable that will be displayed when the **Show_Events** property is set to `true` in the tool pane. This code is not required for all Web Parts; it is specific to our **Site Navigator** example, which is designed to show trace information.

Add the code in Listing 5.3 to the Site Navigator's **WebPart** class.

```
private string Message;
protected override void CreateChildControls()
{
        Message += "CreateChildControls <br/>";
        base.CreateChildControls ();
}
protected override void OnDataBinding(EventArgs e)
{
        base.OnDataBinding (e);
        Message += "OnDataBinding - Server is binding datasources
                ➲ and controls if needed.</br>";
}
protected override void OnInit(EventArgs e)
{
        base.OnInit (e);
        Message += "OnInit - Control is initializing</br>";
}
protected override void OnLoad(EventArgs e)
{
        base.OnLoad (e);
        Message += "OnLoad - Control is loading into page<br>";
}
protected override void OnPreRender(EventArgs e)
{
        base.OnPreRender (e);
        Message += "OnPreRender -  Control is ready to start
                ➲ rendering<br/>";
}
protected override void OnUnload(EventArgs e)
{
        base.OnUnload (e);
        Message += "OnUnload - Control is unloading - this happens
                ➲ after the control is rendered and will not be seen
                ➲ on the screen<br/>";
}
```

**Listing 5.3:** Web Part Events.

## Modify the RenderWebPart Method

The **RenderWebPart** method creates the HTML that describes the Web Part to the browser. To render the Web Part, the **RenderWebPart** method of the **WebPart** class must be overridden, which the **Web Part Library** template does automatically. You must modify the overridden **RenderWebPart** method as follows.

To modify the **WebPart** class's **RenderWebPart** method:

1.  Use the following syntax to remove any default content from the **RenderWebPart** method, but leave the method declaration:

    ```
    protected override void RenderWebPart
    ➲ (HtmlTextWriter output){   }
    ```

2.  Use the methods available to the **HtmlTextWriter** class to send HTML to the output buffer, which will send it on to the client. For more information on methods available to the **HtmlTextWriter** class, see Chapter 8.

    In Chapter 4, we used the HtmlTextWriter's **Write** method. The **Write** method simply takes whatever is sent to it and writes it to the output buffer. Our **Site Navigator** example uses a stack-based output scheme. The HtmlTextWriter's **RenderBeginTag** will output the correct HTML opening tag based on the method's parameter. The **RenderEndTag**, which takes no parameter, will output the HTML closing tags in the reverse order of their rendering.

    Listing 5.4 displays the **RenderWebPart** method for the **Site Navigator** Web Part.

    ```
    protected override void RenderWebPart(HtmlTextWriter output)
    {
            string[,] Sites = GetSiteList();

            Context.Trace.Warn("Tracing","RenderWebPart - Creating
                ➲ the output");
    ```

```
Message += "RenderWebPart - Creating the output<br/>";
output.AddAttribute ("width", "90%");
output.RenderBeginTag(HtmlTextWriterTag.Table); //table
//loop the array adding a row to the table for each
int uBound = Sites.GetUpperBound(0);
for(int x = 0;x<=uBound;x++)
{
        output.RenderBeginTag(HtmlTextWriterTag.Tr);
        output.RenderBeginTag (HtmlTextWriterTag.Td);

        //creating the anchor tag with
        // an href attribute
        output.AddAttribute
            (HtmlTextWriterAttribute.Href,
              ➲ Sites[x,1]);
        output.RenderBeginTag(HtmlTextWriterTag.A);
        //link text
        output.Write (Sites[x,0]);
        output.RenderEndTag (); //close A tag
        output.RenderEndTag();   //close td

        output.RenderBeginTag(HtmlTextWriterTag.Td);
        //Description of site
        output.Write(Sites[x,2]);
        output.RenderEndTag(); //close td
        output.RenderEndTag();   //close tr
}
output.RenderEndTag() ; //close table

if (Show _ Events)
{
output.Write("<br/><br/>");
output.Write(Message);
}
    }
```

**Listing 5.4:** The Site Navigator Web Part's RenderWebPart Method.

3. Save the project.

4. Build the **Web Part Control Library** project in the virtual server's bin directory by selecting **Build** ⇨ **Build Solution** from the Visual Studio .NET menu. The project will be checked for errors. If no errors are present, building the project will result in an assembly stored at the location of the **Output Path** property.

## Modifying the Web Part Definition File

The Web Part definition file (.dwp) details Web Part properties, as well as the location of the Web Part's assembly and its type name. The definition file is created by the **Web Part Library** template and is named WebPart1.dwp by default.

1. In Visual Studio .NET's **Solution Explorer** pane, give the WebPart1.dwp file a more descriptive name by right-clicking the file and selecting the **Rename** menu item. Changing the default file name will make the definition file name easier to identify when importing the file into a Web Part page or a library. For this example, change the name of the WebPart1.dwp file to SiteNav.dwp.

2. Modify the Web Part definition file's XML. Because the XML in the definition file is specific to each Web Part instance, you must modify the definition file to match the Web Part.

   Listing 5.5 shows the **Site Navigator** definition file after it has been modified.

```
<?xml version="1.0" encoding="utf-8"?>
<WebPart xmlns="http://schemas.microsoft.com/
       WebPart/v2" >
       <Title>Site Navigator</Title>
       <Description>The Site Navigator will display links
              to subsites</Description>
       <Assembly>RationalPressWebParts</Assembly>

       <TypeName>RationalPress.WebParts.
              SiteNavigator</TypeName>
```

```
<!-- Specify initial values for any additional
                ➲ base class or custom properties here. -->
</WebPart>
```

**Listing 5.5:** Modified Definition File for the Site Navigator Web Part.

3.   Save the modified definition file.

## Marking the Web Part Safe to Render

For a Web Part to run, it must be listed as safe in the SafeControls section of the
`web.config` file. Mark the Web Part as safe to render, as described in Chapter
4.

## Deploying the Web Part

Once the Web Part has been built, the definition file modified, and the Web Part
marked as safe to render in the `web.config` file, the Web Part definition file can
be imported and added to a page, as described in Chapter 4. Once the Web Part
renders its content to a page successfully, the user can modify custom properties
in the tool pane, and view the simple trace information that the **Site Navigator**
Web Part provides.

*Bonus:*

Once you register this book at www.rationalpress.com, you can download the code in
this chapter (in both Visual C# and Visual Basic .NET) free of charge.

# Chapter 6

# Code Access Security

Code Access Security (CAS) is one of the strengths of the .NET Framework, providing a more granular approach to security than the access security models offered in the pre-.NET era. Before CAS, permissions for such privileged operations as file I/O adopted an "all or nothing" approach, based on the context of the process, regardless of the origin of the request. CAS allows privileges to be based on where the code is loaded from and who wrote the code. Privileges are no longer based solely on user ID. A user accessing an application located on a local machine can have more privileges than he or she would have when accessing the application remotely.

Because Web Parts and the Web Part infrastructure sit atop ASP .NET, they participate in CAS like any other .NET code. We saw a bit of CAS in Chapter 5, when we set the **trust** element in the `web.config` file to **WSS_Medium**, enabling the Web Part to access the SharePoint object model. Granting a blanket increase in permissions to the virtual server is discouraged: the more targeted the security, the better. In this chapter, we will look at the additional *permission sets* used with WSS and SPS, as well as ways to allow the minimum amount of access necessary for a Web Part to function.

# What is Code Access Security?

While this book is not about CAS specifically, it is important to understand a little about CAS's function and importance. CAS is part of the .NET Framework, and all .NET code participates in CAS. CAS provides a security layer that verifies that the code is allowed to access such privileged operations as file I/O and database access. ASP .NET's CAS setting is configured by the **trust** element in the web.config file. The **trust** element's **level** attribute specifies the named permission set for the virtual server. A named permission set contains one or more permissions and can be referenced by name. Named permission sets allow an administrator to associate one or more permissions with a section or sections of code, using the permission set name to indicate what privileged operations are allowed. For example, an administrator might allow file I/O but disallow writing to the registry. Some of the possible privileges are:

▶ **SqlClientPermission** — Allows code access to the SQL Server.

▶ **DirectoryServicesPermission** — Allows code access to Directory Services.

▶ **DnsPermission** — Allows code to query domain name services.

▶ **FileIOPermission** — Allows code to read/write files.

▶ **RegistryPermission** — Allows code to read/write registries.

▶ **WebPermission** — Allows code to make a web connection.

The .NET Framework installs with five named permission sets, each allowing progressively fewer privileges:

▶ Full

▶ High

▶ Medium

▶ Low

▶ Minimal

In general, it is best to allow only the minimal privileges necessary for Web Parts to accomplish their required tasks.

# CAS Permissions and Trust Levels

WSS installs with two new permissions: **SharePointPermission** and **WebPartPermission**. These new permissions are classes that exist in `Microsoft.SharePoint.Security.dll` and participate in CAS.

**SharePointPermission** has the following attributes:

▶ **ObjectModel** — Allows access to the WSS/SPS object model.

▶ **UnsafeSaveOnGet** — Allows saving to the underlying databases on HTTP **Get** requests.

▶ **Unrestricted** — Allows access to the WSS/SPS Object Model and saving to the underlying database on HTTP **Get** requests.

**WebPartPermission** has the following attributes:

▶ **Connections** — Permits a Web Part to participate in Web Part connections.

▶ **Unrestricted** — Permits a Web Part to perform any privileged operation controlled by **WebPartPermission**. Since there is only one privileged operation listed in **WebPartPermission**, the **Unrestricted** attribute functions identically to the **Connections** attribute.

A Web Part may not access any privileged resources or operations without the necessary permissions. WSS installs two trust levels on the server: **WSS_Minimal** and **WSS_Medium**. The default trust level for the virtual server is **WSS_Minimal**. Table 6.1 lists the permissions for **WSS_Minimal** and **WSS_Medium**.

| PERMISSION | WSS_MINIMAL | WSS_MEDIUM |
|---|---|---|
| Environment | Access Unavailable | Allows TEMP, TMP, OS, USERNAME, COMPUTERNAME permissions. |
| FileIO | Access Unavailable | Allows Read, Write, Append, PathDiscovery: Application Directory permissions. |
| IsolatedStorage | Access Unavailable | Allows AssemblyIsolationByUser and UserQuota permissions. |
| Security | Allows Execution | Allows Execution, Assertion, ControlPrincipal, ControlThread, RemotingConfiguration permissions. |
| WebPermission | Access Unavailable | Allows connection to origin host (requires configuration of URLs). |
| DNS | Access Unavailable | Unrestricted (all sub permissions granted). |
| Printing | Access Unavailable | Allows default printing. |
| SqlClientPermission | Access Unavailable | Unrestricted (all sub permissions granted). |
| SharePointPermission | Access Unavailable | Allows ObjectModel permission. |
| WebPartPermission | Allows access to WebPartPermission.Connections | Allows Connections permission. |

**Table 6.1:** WSS_Minimal and WSS_Medium Trust Levels and Permissions.

## Setting the Correct Trust Level

In Chapter 5, we changed the **level** attribute of the **trust** element from **WSS_Minimal** to **WSS_Medium**. This increase in privileges granted our **Site Navigator** Web Part access to the WSS object model. If the **Site Navigator** Web Part example (or any Web Part requiring access to the WSS Object Model) is already imported into a Web Part page without an increase in privileges, the Web Part will throw a security exception when it tries to access the WSS Object Model. If the calling code in the Web Part does not trap the resultant exception, the Web Part infrastructure will be forced to handle it, as shown in Figure 6.1. If this occurs, the user will not have access to any Web Parts.

**Figure 6.1:** Security Exception Handled by the Web Part infrastructure.

Any code that may not possess the required permissions in all circumstances should be designed to catch and handle security exceptions. Catching security exceptions and displaying error messages gracefully allows the page to continue to render and the user to continue to interact with other Web Parts. Changing the trust level to **Full** effectively bypasses many CAS permission checks for assemblies running within the virtual server. It is generally not a good policy to provide open access to all code running within the virtual server.

For Web Parts that require access to protected resources, there are three possible configurations to enable them to run without throwing exceptions:

- ▶ Increasing the virtual server's trust level

- ▶ Installing the Web Part assembly into the Global Assembly Cache (GAC)

- ▶ Creating a custom policy file for the Web Part assembly

You can implement any of these solutions to increase the privileges for a Web Part assembly. Deciding which solution to implement must be based on your environment.

*Tech Tip:*

Creating a custom policy file is the recommended solution for a production environment that must allow Web Parts to access protected code. It is always a good idea to minimize the privileges of specific assemblies and limit the ability of bad code to create problems.

Let's look at the advantages and drawbacks of all three possible solutions.

## Increasing the Virtual Server's Trust Level

One method of enabling a Web Part to access protected resources without returning errors is to increase the trust level for the virtual server. Changing the virtual server's trust level from **WSS_Minimal** to a more trusting setting— like **WSS_Medium** or **Full** — increases the trust level for *all* assemblies. Generally speaking, you should avoid this, with the possible exception of work done on an isolated development server. When developing Web Parts, it is sometimes easiest to simply raise the trust level of the virtual server. Be aware, however, that bugs may surface during deployment, since the configuration these Web Parts are built on is not recommended for a production environment. Always use caution when increasing the trust level on a development server, since a Web Part will generally be deployed at a higher security setting on a production server and might not run as expected.

For more information on how to increase the trust level of the virtual server, see Chapter 5.

## Installing the Web Part Assembly into the Global Assembly Cache

Another method of enabling a Web Part to access protected resources without returning errors is to deploy the Web Part assembly into the Global Assembly Cache (GAC). To do so, the assembly must be signed with a *strong name*. (A strong name is a name that contains the text name, version number, culture information, and public key token. Signing an assembly with a strong name gives the assembly a unique identity.) Installing an assembly into the GAC automatically grants the assembly full trust. The benefit of installing into the GAC is that the virtual server can be configured at a lower trust level, and only the assemblies requiring higher trust levels receive increased permissions. The problem with deploying to the GAC is that the assembly receives *all* privileges— not just those it requires. Deploying to the GAC may be a better solution than increasing the permissions on the virtual server, but it still provides more access than a Web Part generally requires.

For procedures on how to install a Web Part assembly into the GAC, and effectively give the Web Part full trust, see Chapter 11.

## Creating a Custom Policy File for the Web Part Assembly

The recommended solution for providing the least amount of privileges to a specific assembly is to create a custom policy file to define a custom permission set. Creating a custom policy file is usually the best solution for assigning the most granular and targeted permissions. A policy file is an XML file that holds permission set information that is used by the .NET Framework to provide CAS. For example, WSS 2.0 ships with two default permission sets: **WSS_Minimal** and **WSS_Medium**. Each of these has its own policy file, which you do not need to alter or modify. However, if you create your own custom permission sets, you must create a custom policy file for each custom permission set. You must also modify the `web.config` file to locate your new custom policy files.

In this section, we will create a custom policy file, target the assembly for membership in the permission set, and set the correct trust level for the virtual server. The result will be a policy file that allows a specific assembly to access the WSS Object Model without elevating the privileges of all other assemblies.

To create a custom policy file and target the assembly for membership in a permission set:

1   Create a copy of the WSS_MinimalTrust policy file to use as a starting point. This file is located at `<root>\Program Files\ Common Files\Microsoft Shared\web server extensions\60\ CONFIG\wss _ minimaltrust.config`. Using Explorer, copy `wss _ minimaltrust.config` and rename the copy to your custom policy's name. For this example, copy `wss _ minimaltrust.config` and rename the file `RationalPressMinimalCustom.config`.

2   Add a **SharePointPermission SecurityClass** element to the **SecurityClasses** element, located under `\configuration\mscorlib\ security\policy\PolicyLevel\`. Use Notepad or an XML editor to open the custom policy file and add the **SecurityClass** element for **SharePointPermission**.

**SYNTAX**

```
<SecurityClass
    Name="<Name of the class that implements the security
      permission>"
    Description="<description of the security class" />
```

**EXAMPLE**

```
<SecurityClass
    Name="SharePointPermission"
    Description="Microsoft.SharePoint.Security.
      SharePointPermission, Microsoft.SharePoint.Security,
      Version=11.0.0.0, Culture=neutral,
      PublicKeyToken=71e9bce111e9429c" />
```

3   Create a new permission set by specifying a **PermissionSet** element and an **IPermission** element. These elements are specified in the `\configuration\mscorlib\security\policy\PolicyLevel\ NamedPermissionSets\` hierarchy, with a **name** attribute of ASP .NET. Add the SharePointPermission's **IPermission** element as shown in the following example.

**SYNTAX**

```
<PermissionSet
   class ="NamedPermissionSet"
   version="<version of the permission set>"
   Name="<friendly name>">
   Description="<description of PermissionSet>"
<IPermission
   class="<class name of permission>"
   version="version number"
   <permission name>="<value>" />
</PermissionSet>
```

**EXAMPLE**

```
<PermissionSet
   class="NamedPermissionSet"
   version="1"
   Name="RationalPress">
<IPermission
   class="AspNetHostingPermission"
   version="1"
   Level="Minimal" />
<IPermission
   class="SecurityPermission"
   version="1"
   Flags="Execution" />
<IPermission
   class="WebPartPermission"
   version="1"
   Connections="True" />
<IPermission
   class="SharePointPermission"
   version="1"
   ObjectModel="True" />
</PermissionSet>
```

The **AspNetHostingPermission** class contains the base to create the new permission set. Adding the **IPermission** element for the **SharePointPermission** class allows access to the SharePoint object model.

4   Create a new **CodeGroup** element, as specified in the hierarchy `\configuration\mscorlib\security\policy\PolicyLevel\ CodeGroup\`. The new **CodeGroup** element will associate the new permission set with the specific assembly. For this example, `RationalPressWebParts.dll` is included as a member of the **CodeGroup** element.

**SYNTAX**

```
<CodeGroup
     class="Assembly that implements the code group"
     version="<version number>"
     PermissionSetName="<Name of the Permission Set>"
   <IMembershipCondition
     class="<Assembly that implements the membership
     condition>"
     version="<version number>"
     <type of membership condition>="<value>" />
</CodeGroup>
```

**EXAMPLE**

```
<CodeGroup
     class="UnionCodeGroup"
     version="1"
     PermissionSetName="RationalPress">
     <IMembershipCondition
     class="UrlMembershipCondition"
     version="1"
     Url="$AppDirUrl$/bin/RationalPressWebParts.dll" />
</CodeGroup>
```

5   Save and close the policy file.

The WSS_RationalPressMinimalCustom.config file associates the **RationalPress** permission set with RationalPressWebParts.dll, which contains the **Site Navigator** Web Part. Only RationalPressWebParts.dll will be able to access the WSS Object Model.

The next step is to tell ASP .NET where to find the custom policy file and configure ASP .NET to use it.

To make a custom policy available to ASP .NET:

1   Open the web.config file for the virtual server. The web.config file for the default virtual server is usually located at <root>\inetpub\ wwwroot\.

2   Add a new **trustLevel** element to the **securityPolicy** element located at \configuration\system.web\ in the web.config file. Using Notepad or another XML editor, add a new **trustLevel** element with the **name** attribute set to the name of the custom policy file and the **policyFile** attribute set to the policy file location in the file system. For this example, set the **name** attribute to the name of our custom policy, **WSS_RPress_Minimal**. The **policyFile** attribute is set to the file location.

**SYNTAX**

```
<securityPolicy>...
    <trustLevel
        name="<Name of the custom security policy>"
        policyFile="location of the policy file" />
</securityPolicy>
```

**EXAMPLE**

```
<securityPolicy>...
    <trustLevel
        name="WSS_RPress_Minimal"
        policyFile="C:\Program Files\Common Files\
        Microsoft Shared\Web Server Extensions\60\config\
        wss_RationalPressMinimalCustom.config" />
</securityPolicy>
```

3    Set the **level** attribute of the **trust** element under `\configuration\` `system.web\` to the **name** attribute of the **trustLevel** tag created in step 2. For the present example, set the **level** attribute to `WSS_` `RPress_Minimal`.

**SYNTAX**
```
<trust level="<name of the custom policy" originUrl="" />
```

**EXAMPLE**
```
<trust level="WSS_RPress_Minimal" originUrl="" />
```

4    Restart IIS to apply the new policy settings.

The **Site Navigator** Web Part is now the only Web Part installed in the `bin` directory that can access the WSS Object Model.

## Testing the Trust Level

To test the trust level, open a WSS or SPS site that contains the **Site Navigator** Web Part. **Site Navigator** uses the WSS Object Model and resides in the **RationalPressWebParts.dll** library. If this assembly is located in the `bin` directory, it should have sufficient privileges to access the SharePoint Object Model. If the Site Navigator assembly is located in the `bin` directory and not the GAC, and renders without raising a security exception, you can conclude that the RationalPressWebParts assembly has the necessary permissions to access the SharePoint Object Model.

*Bonus:*

The custom policy file `WSS_RationalPressMinimalCustom.config` **and the new Site Navigator Web Part are available for download after you register this book at** `www.rationalpress.com`.

# Advanced Topics

# Chapter 7

# Debugging Web Parts

Like any other piece of .NET code, Web Parts can be debugged and traced. *Debugging* is the process of detecting, locating, and correcting errors. *Tracing* is the ability to execute code in a way that allows a sequence of executed statements to be observed so that they can be debugged.

This chapter shows how to configure WSS and SPS to allow tracing and debugging. The first section, "Tracing a Web Part," shows how to add custom messages to the tracing output. The second section, "Debugging a Web Part," demonstrates how to attach and use the debugger to debug the Web Part.

## *Tracing a Web Part*

Tracing a Web Part can provide a lot of information about how the Web Part works and how the code progresses during execution. Enabling tracing for the virtual server returns information about:

- ▶ Controls on the page
- ▶ Request Header
- ▶ Code execution path
- ▶ ViewState
- ▶ Server variables

## Enabling Tracing on the Virtual Server

To access trace information, tracing must be enabled on the virtual server. To enable tracing on the virtual server, follow these steps:

1.  Using Notepad, open the `web.config` file located in the virtual server's root directory, which is usually `<root>\inetpub\wwwroot`.

2.  Find the **trace** element by choosing **Edit** ⇨ **Find**. Enter `trace` in the text box and click the **Find Next** button.

3.  Set the **enabled** attribute of the **trace** element to `true`. The **trace** element is located in the `configuration/system.web` section and should now look like the following:

    ```
    <trace enabled='true' pageOutput='true' localOnly='true'/>
    ```

4.  Find the **trust** element in the `web.config` file and make sure the level is set to at least **WSS_Medium**. A trust level below **WSS_Medium** does not allow tracing. For details on trust levels and Code Access Security, see Chapter 6.

5.  Save the `web.config` file.

The next page rendered by the server will include trace information, which is located at the bottom of the page and visible only on the local machine. Setting the **localOnly** attribute to `false` allows trace information for remote browsers, which could pose a security risk by allowing everyone to view trace information.

| Request Details | | | |
|---|---|---|---|
| Session Id: | | Request Type: | GET |
| Time of Request: | 8/7/2004 2:25:17 PM | Status Code: | 200 |
| Request Encoding: | Unicode (UTF-8) | Response Encoding: | Unicode (UTF-8) |

| Trace Information | | | |
|---|---|---|---|
| Category | Message | From First(s) | From Last(s) |
| aspx.page | Begin Init | | |
| aspx.page | End Init | 0.000164 | 0.000164 |
| aspx.page | Begin PreRender | 0.000357 | 0.000194 |
| aspx.page | End PreRender | 0.007987 | 0.007629 |
| aspx.page | Begin SaveViewState | 0.008779 | 0.000793 |
| aspx.page | End SaveViewState | 0.008854 | 0.000075 |
| aspx.page | Begin Render | 0.008914 | 0.000060 |
| aspx.page | End Render | 0.010688 | 0.001774 |

| Control Tree | | Render Size Bytes (including children) | Viewstate Size Bytes (excluding children) |
|---|---|---|---|
| Control Id | Type | | |
| __PAGE | ASP.default_aspx | 31643 | 20 |
| _ctl0 | Microsoft.SharePoint.WebControls.ProjectProperty | 32 | 0 |
| _ctl1 | Microsoft.SharePoint.WebControls.Theme | 0 | 0 |
| _ctl2 | Microsoft.SharePoint.WebControls.Navigation | 579 | 0 |
| _ctl3 | Microsoft.SharePoint.WebControls.PortalConnection | 66 | 0 |
| _ctl4 | Microsoft.SharePoint.WebControls.ProjectProperty | 32 | 0 |
| L_SearchView | Microsoft.SharePoint.WebControls.ViewSearchForm | 0 | 0 |
| _ctl5 | Microsoft.SharePoint.WebPartPages.SettingsLink | 423 | 0 |
| _ctl6 | Microsoft.SharePoint.WebPartPages.AuthenticationButton | 0 | 0 |
| _ctl7 | Microsoft.SharePoint.WebControls.Navigation | 334 | 0 |
| _ctl8 | Microsoft.SharePoint.WebControls.Navigation | 0 | 0 |
| _ctl9 | Microsoft.SharePoint.WebControls.Navigation | 574 | 0 |
| _ctl10 | Microsoft.SharePoint.WebControls.Navigation | 338 | 0 |

**Figure 7.1:** Viewing Trace Information.

## *Adding Content to the Trace Information*

The **Context** object contains the properties about the HTTP request that started the page generation. You can use the **Trace** property of the **Context** object to add content to the trace information. The **Trace** property is actually a **System.Web. TraceContext** object. Content can be added to the trace information using the **Trace** object's **Warn** and **Write** methods. The main difference between these methods is that the **Warn** method displays in red.

To add and view trace content from the Web Part, follow these steps:

1.  Make sure that tracing is enabled on the virtual server, as described in the "Enabling Tracing on the Virtual Server" section of this chapter.

2.  Modify the **WebPart** class by adding a **Trace.Warn** or **Trace. Write** method call, passing in a string value for the message. The **Trace** object for the page can be accessed from the **Context** object.

To see an example, let's add content to the trace information by adding **Trace. Warn** method calls to the **Site Navigator** Web Part we created in Chapter 5. To modify the **Site Navigator** Web Part, follow these steps:

1.  In Visual Studio .NET, select **File** ➪ **Open** ➪ **Project**, and navigate to the solution (.sln) file for the **Site Navigator** project. For example, navigate to: C:\WebParts\C5\RationalPressWebPart\ RationalPressWebParts.sln. This path depends on where the solution file is located.

2.  Use the following syntax to add the **Warn** method call, which will add a message to the trace information.

**SYNTAX**

```
Context.Trace.Warn(string category, string message);
```

**EXAMPLE**

```
Context.Trace.Warn("Site _ Nav", "OnInit - Control is
        ➲ initializing");
```

The **category** parameter groups the messages and is displayed in the trace information section in the first column, titled **Category**.

3.  From the **Visual Studio** menu, choose **Build** ⇨ **Rebuild Solution** to rebuild the solution and create a new assembly.

4.  Refresh your browser or browse to a page with the updated **Site Navigator** Web Part. The trace information should be located at the bottom of the page.

Figure 7.2 displays the trace output, showing content from our example Web Part.

**Request Details**

| Session Id: | | Request Type: | GET |
|---|---|---|---|
| Time of Request: | 8/7/2004 2:41:28 PM | Status Code: | 200 |
| Request Encoding: | Unicode (UTF-8) | Response Encoding: | Unicode (UTF-8) |

**Trace Information**

| Category | Message | From First(s) | From Last(s) |
|---|---|---|---|
| aspx.page | Begin Init | | |
| aspx.page | End Init | 0.000259 | 0.000259 |
| Site_Nav | OnInit - Control is initializing | 0.001362 | 0.001102 |
| Site_Nav | OnLoad - Control is loading into page | 0.001720 | 0.000358 |
| aspx.page | Begin PreRender | 0.001793 | 0.000073 |
| Site_Nav | CreateChildControls | 0.043476 | 0.041683 |
| Site_Nav | OnPreRender - Control is ready to start rendering | 0.043909 | 0.000433 |
| aspx.page | End PreRender | 0.043963 | 0.000054 |
| aspx.page | Begin SaveViewState | 0.044667 | 0.000703 |
| aspx.page | End SaveViewState | 0.044776 | 0.000110 |
| aspx.page | Begin Render | 0.044819 | 0.000043 |
| Site_Nav | RenderWebPart - Creating the output | 0.050248 | 0.005429 |
| Site_Nav | GetSiteList | 0.051223 | 0.000975 |
| Site_Nav | GetSiteList - Webs = 5 | 0.258734 | 0.207510 |
| aspx.page | End Render | 0.538868 | 0.280134 |

**Control Tree**

| Control Id | Type | Render Size Bytes (including children) | Viewstate Size Bytes (excluding children) |
|---|---|---|---|
| __PAGE | ASP.default_aspx | 38460 | 20 |
| _ctl0 | Microsoft.SharePoint.WebControls.ProjectProperty | 9 | 0 |
| _ctl1 | Microsoft.SharePoint.WebControls.Theme | 0 | 0 |
| _ctl2 | Microsoft.SharePoint.WebControls.Navigation | 535 | 0 |
| _ctl3 | Microsoft.SharePoint.WebControls.PortalConnection | 0 | 0 |

**Figure 7.2:** Site Navigator Trace Output.

# *Debugging a Web Part*

Tracing displays the execution path *after* the code has executed. Debugging, on the other hand, allows you to step though the code *as it executes*. While debugging, you can view the *Call Stack*, view and modify variables, and set *breakpoints*. The Call Stack is a debugging tool that displays the methods that the code has stepped through. Breakpoints are halting points that you can set. When you are debugging, execution stops at each breakpoint until it is allowed to continue.

Visual Studio .NET provides a debugger and many tools, like the Call Stack, that can be used to step though Web Part code in the same way you can step through an ASP .NET web page. Debugging involves modifying the web.config file to allow the application to be debugged and attaching the debugger to the **w3wp.exe** process. The **w3wp.exe** process is the process that hosts ASP .NET.

## *Modifying the web.config File for Debugging*

Before you can step through the Web Part code, you must modify the web.config file as described in the following steps:

1. Using Notepad, open the web.config file located in the virtual server's root directory, which is usually <root>:\inetpub\ wwwroot.

2. Find the **SafeMode** element by choosing **Edit** ➪ **Find**. Enter SafeMode in the text box and click the **Find Next** button.

3. Set the **CallStack** attribute of the **SafeMode** element to true. The **CallStack** attribute determines whether Call Stack information will be displayed on an exception.

4. Find the **compilation** element and set the **debug** attribute to true. The **debug** attribute determines whether debugging is allowed.

5. Find the **customErrors** element and set the **mode** attribute to Off. When **customErrors** is set to On, true debug information is hidden from the end user. Setting **customErrors** to Off allows the error message to be displayed.

6. Find the **trust** element and make sure the level is set to at least **WSS_Medium**. A trust level below **WSS_Medium** does not allow debugging. For details on trust levels and Code Access Security, see Chapter 6.

7. Save the web.config file.

## Setting a Breakpoint

A breakpoint temporarily halts execution and allows you to use various debugging tools. To set a breakpoint:

1.  In Visual Studio .NET, choose **File** ⇨ **Open** ⇨ **Project** to display the **Open Project** dialog box. Browse to the solution (.sln) file for the **Web Part Library** project.

    For example, browse to the **Site Navigator** project you created in Chapter 5. The Web Part project will open in Visual Studio .NET.

2.  Right-click a line of code and select **Insert Breakpoint** from the pop-up menu.

    For example, open the WebParts.cs file of the **SiteNavigator** class and locate the **RenderWebPart** method. Right-click a line of executable code, and select **Insert Breakpoint** from the pop-up menu. This creates a breakpoint on the selected line of code.

Figure 7.3 shows the **RenderWebPart** method with a breakpoint set highlighted.

```
output.AddAttribute ("width", "90%");
output.RenderBeginTag(HtmlTextWriterTag.Table); //table tag

//loop the array adding a row to the table for each
int uBound = Sites.GetUpperBound(0);
for(int x = 0;x<=uBound;x++)
{
    output.RenderBeginTag(HtmlTextWriterTag.Tr);
    output.RenderBeginTag (HtmlTextWriterTag.Td);
    //creating the anchor tag with an href attribute
    output.AddAttribute (HtmlTextWriterAttribute.Href,Sites[x,1]);
    output.RenderBeginTag(HtmlTextWriterTag.A);
    //link text
    output.Write (Sites[x,0]);
    output.RenderEndTag (); //close A tag
    output.RenderEndTag();  //close td
    output.RenderBeginTag(HtmlTextWriterTag.Td);
    //Description of site
    output.Write(Sites[x,2]);
    output.RenderEndTag(); //close td
    output.RenderEndTag();  //close tr
}
output.RenderEndTag() ; //close table

if (Show_Events)
{
    output.Write("<br/><br/>");
    output.Write(Message);
```

**Figure 7.3:** RenderWebPart Method with Breakpoint.

## *Attaching the Debugger*

There are two ways to attach the debugger to the process that hosts the assembly. The first way is to provide a start-up page for the Web Part project. When Visual Studio .NET runs the code in Debug Mode, it will attach the debugger to the process that is running the start-up page. Since the Web Part is part of a web page, the debugger will be attached to the **w3wp.exe** process.

The second way to attach a debugger is to attach it manually to one or more process. This method allows you to attach the debugger to an existing process.

Attaching the debugger using the start-up page always creates a new page. Manually attaching the debugger requires that the **w3wp.exe** process is already running.

### *Attaching a Debugger Using a Start-up Page*

This method of debugging a Web Part automatically attaches the debugger and opens the start-up page in Internet Explorer.

1.  In Visual Studio .NET, choose **Project** ⇨ **<your project's name> Properties** to access your project properties. For example, if you are working with the **RationalPressWebParts** project, select **RationalPressWebParts Properties**. The project's **Property Pages** window will be displayed.

2.  From the left pane of the **Property Pages** dialog box, select **Configuration Properties** ⇨ **Debugging**. The **Debug Mode** value is listed under the **Start Action** section. Figure 7.4 shows the project's **Property Pages** dialog box with the Debug Mode set to URL. Modify the project's Debug mode by setting **Debug Mode** to URL. The Debug Mode for the project determines how to start the project when debugging. This project will start by navigating to a specific URL which should contain an instance of a Web Part to debug.

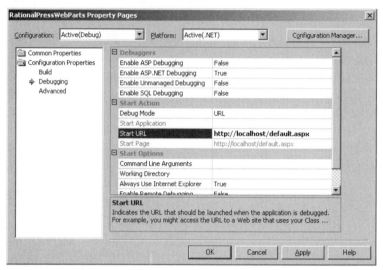

**Figure 7.4:** Project Property Pages Dialog Box.

3.   Set the **Start URL** property to a page that contains the Web Part to be debugged. For example, set the **Start URL** property to `http://localhost/default.aspx`. This page contains the **Site Navigator** Web Part, which is the project opened in Visual Studio .NET.

4.   Make sure that **Enable ASP .NET Debugging** is set to `True`. This value is set in the **Debuggers** pane of the project's **Property Pages** dialog box, as shown in Figure 7.4.

5.   Run the Web Part from the Visual Studio .NET interface. From Visual Studio's top-level menu, select **Debug ➪ Run**. Visual Studio will open a browser to the location defined in the **Start URL** property and attach the debugger to the correct **w3wp.exe** process. The code will run until the breakpoint is reached, at which point the debugger will temporarily halt execution.

6.   While the code is halted at a breakpoint, you can view variables and Call Stack information, as well as run code in the Visual Studio .NET **Immediate** pane. From Visual Studio .NET's top-level menu, choose **Debug ➪ Continue** to continue the code execution. The debugger will resume code execution until it encounters another breakpoint or ends.

## *Manually Attaching the Debugger*

You can attach the debugger to a running process from within Visual Studio .NET by using the **Processes** dialog box. This technique allows you to attach the debugger to a running process, such as a **w3wp.exe** process that is processing the page with a Web Part. The code that will be debugged must have been built with debug information. If you build a Web Part project while in Debug configuration, the compiler will include the debug information. To determine if the compiler is including the necessary debug information, look in the output path location (in our example, the virtual server's `bin` directory) for a .pdb file with the same name as the assembly. If the Web Part was built under a configuration that is not set to produce the necessary debugging information, you will need to rebuild the Web Part in Debug configuration to debug it. Refer to the .NET Framework and Visual Studio Help files for more information about project configurations.

To manually select the process and attach the debugger:

1. Select **Debug** ➪ **Processes** from the Visual Studio top-level menu. The **Processes** dialog box will be displayed, as shown in Figure 7.5.

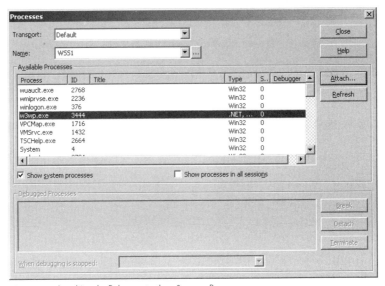

**Figure 7.5:** Attaching the Debugger to the w3wp.exe Process.

2.  Make sure that the **Show system processes** check box is selected. This allows the system process to be displayed in the **Available Processes** list.

3.  Select the **w3wp.exe** process and click the **Attach** button.

 *Caution:*

You may find more than one w3wp.exe process running. It may be difficult to determine which process to select, and there is no sure way to know, unless you pick one and debug it.

4.  In the **Attach to Process** dialog box, click the **Common Language Runtime** check box, then click the **OK** button. This tells the debugger to debug .NET code.

*Tech Tip:*

If the w3wp.exe process is not in the list of processes, either the **Show system processes** check box is not selected or the w3wp.exe process is not running. First, make sure that **Show system processes** is checked. If the w3wp.exe process still does not appear, then it is probably not running. You can start it by making a request to a page hosted on the w3wp server. Click the **Refresh** button and the process will be listed.

5.  Close the **Processes** dialog box.

6.  In a web browser, navigate to a page that contains the Web Part that is open in Visual Studio .NET. The debugger will halt execution on the breakpoint and give control to Visual Studio .NET.

7.  While the code is halted at a breakpoint, you can view variables and Call Stack information, as well as run code in the Visual Studio .NET **Immediate** pane. To continue the code execution, choose **Debug ⇨ Continue** from Visual Studio's top-level menu. The debugger will resume code execution until it encounters another breakpoint or ends.

# Chapter 8

# Using Web Parts to Create HTML

This chapter describes how developers can use methods of the **HtmlTextWriter** object and Web Part child controls to render HTML that will create the most appropriate visual interface on the web page.

On a web page, a Web Part is contained in either a Web Part zone or directly in the content of the web page itself. Web Parts that are contained within a Web Part zone are considered *dynamic*, which means that they participate in all Web Part functionality – such as personalization of properties – without requiring the use of development tools or editors. Web Parts contained directly in a web page are considered *static*, which means that they act like standard ASP .NET server controls and do not participate in all Web Part functionality unless they are modified. Both categories of Web Parts must override the Web Part's **RenderWebPart** virtual method. When rendering the page, ASP .NET will call the **Render** method on the Web Part (which you should not override), as it does for any server control. The **Render** method of the Web Part base class emits the HTML for the border around the Web Part, including the title bar text, border style, extensible Web Part menu, and other UI elements, which can be controlled through properties and methods on the Web Part base class. The **Render** method then calls the Web Part's **RenderWebPart** method to emit the HTML for the body of the Web Part. In this way, the **Render** method on the Web Part base class and the **RenderWebPart** method on the derived child Web Part class work together to create the HTML for the Web Part on the page. As with the **Render** method on server controls, the **RenderWebPart** method accepts one parameter named **output**, which is of type **System.Web.UI.HtmlTextWriter**, which is an ASP .NET class. The **RenderWebPart** method is a part of the Web Part life cycle, which is discussed in more detail in Appendix A.

## Caution:

It is the developer's responsibility to ensure that any user input posted through the web page or any Web Part properties that are modified by personalization will not expose the overall system to dangers from script injection attacks or from SQL injection attacks on the back end system. Any input that comes from an outside source should be regarded as suspect, whether it comes from users or from other applications. One way to minimize the danger is to encode all externally-provided input in HTML by using **SPEncode.HtmlEncode,** or through the use of simple validation techniques. For details on security measures such as HTML-encoding and validating external input, as well as how to limit access to properties, see Appendix C, available online after you register this book at www.rationalpress.com.

# Using the HtmlTextWriter Methods

The **HtmlTextWriter** object is used to write HTML that will ultimately be sent to the client. You can use either of two general categories of **HtmlTextWriter** methods: simple Write methods and stack-based methods.

## Note:

The methods described in this chapter are *overloaded,* which means that they can accept various parameter types. For example, the Write method can accept a string value, integer value, character value, and so on. To see a complete list of methods and parameter options, refer to the .NET Framework Help files.

## Tech Tip:

Use the **SPEncode** class located in the **Microsoft.SharePoint.Utilities** namespace to encode or decode text. Developers should use the **HtmlEncode** method of the **SPEncode** class to convert special HTML characters such as < and > to entities like &lt; and &gt;..

# Using Write Methods

The **HtmlTextWriter** class contains many simple methods to write parameter values to the output stream. These methods provide little or no processing before passing the information to the output stream. The following methods are often used to generate HTML content in the **RenderWebPart** method.

► **Write** – The HtmlTextWriter's **Write** method will place a parameter's value in the output text stream. This method does not append a line break to the output.

**SYNTAX**
```
object.Write(value);
```

**EXAMPLE**
```
output.Write("This has been brought to you by the Write
        ➲ method");
```

► **WriteLine** – The HtmlTextWriter's **WriteLine** method will place a parameter's value in the output text stream. This method will append a line break to the output to force a new line.

**SYNTAX**
```
object.WriteLine(value);
```

**EXAMPLE**
```
output.WriteLine("This has been brought to you by the
        ➲ Writeline method");
```

► **WriteBeginTag** – The HtmlTextWriter's **WriteBeginTag** method will place a begin tag in the output text stream. The begin tag will not have a closing (>) character and will need to be closed properly after any attributes are added. Use the HtmlTextWriter's **TagRightChar** constant to properly close the tag.

**SYNTAX**
```
object.WriteBeginTag (value);
```

**EXAMPLE**

```
output.WriteBeginTag ("Body");
output.Write(HtmlTextWriter TagRightChar);
```

▶ **WriteEndTag** – The HtmlTextWriter's **WriteEndTag** method will place an end tag in the output text stream.

**SYNTAX**

```
object.WriteEndTag (value);
```

**EXAMPLE**

```
output.WriteEndTag ("Body");
```

▶ **WriteAttribute** - The HtmlTextWriter's **WriteAttribute** method will place an attribute and the attribute value in the output text stream.

**SYNTAX**

```
object.WriteAttribute (value, value);
```

**EXAMPLE**

```
output.WriteBeginTag ("table");
output.WriteAttribute ("Border","1");
output.Write(HtmlTextWriter TagRightChar);
```

▶ **WriteStyleAttribute** - The HtmlTextWriter's **WriteStyleAttribute** method will place an HTML **Style** attribute and its value in the output text stream.

**SYNTAX**

```
object.WriteStyleAttribute (value, value);
```

**EXAMPLE**

```
output.WriteBeginTag ("table");
output.WriteStyleAttribute ("BorderColor","Blue");
output.Write(HtmlTextWriter TagRightChar);
```

## Using Stack-Based Methods

The **HtmlTextWriter** class includes *stack-based* methods to create HTML. Stack-based methods operate like a stack-based data structure, where you add tags to the output and then close them in the opposite order. It is a type of "first in, last out" algorithm, which effectively unwinds the stack to add close tags.

The stack-based methods of the **HtmlTextWriter** class are:

▶ **RenderBeginTag** – The HtmlTextWriter's **RenderBeginTag** method will place a begin tag (including the following closing tag (>)) in the output text stream.

**SYNTAX**
```
object.RenderBeginTag (value);
```

**EXAMPLE**
```
output.RenderBeginTag ("table");
```

▶ **RenderEndTag** – The HtmlTextWriter's **RenderEndTag** method will place the next end tag in the stack into the output text stream.

**SYNTAX**
```
object.RenderEndTag ();
```

**EXAMPLE**
```
output.RenderEndTag ();
```

▶ **AddAttribute** – The HtmlTextWriter's **AddAttribute** method will place an attribute and the attribute value in the output text stream. To add an attribute to an element, **AddAttribute** must be called before the **RenderBeginTag** method is called. This is different than the Write methods discussed earlier, where the begin tag is added, followed by the attribute and the **TagRightChar** constant.

**SYNTAX**
```
object.AddAttribute (style value, value);
object.RenderBeginTag (value);
```

**EXAMPLE**
```
output.AddAttribute ("Border","1");
output.RenderBeginTag ("table");
```

▶ **AddStyleAttribute** – The HtmlTextWriter's **AddStyleAttribute** method will place an HTML **Style** attribute and its value in the output text stream. To add a **Style** attribute to an element, **AddStyleAttribute** must be called before the **RenderBeginTag** method is called. This is different than the Write methods discussed earlier, where the begin tag is added, followed by the attribute and the **TagRightChar** constant.

**SYNTAX**

```
object.AddStyleAttribute (style value, value);
```

**EXAMPLE**

```
output.AddStyleAttribute ("BorderColor","Blue");
output.RenderBeginTag ("table");
```

It is easier to understand the stack-based nature of these methods by looking at a longer example. Listing 8.1 shows a longer example of using the stack-based methods.

```
protected override void RenderWebPart(HtmlTextWriter output)
{
    output.AddAttribute("Border","1");
    output.AddAttribute("width","100%");
    output.RenderBeginTag("Table");
    output.RenderBeginTag("Tr");
    output.RenderBeginTag("Td");
    output.Write("Cell 1 Data");
    output.RenderEndTag            //closes the Td tag
    output.RenderBeginTag("Td");
    output.Write("Cell 2 Data");
    output.RenderEndTag            //closes the Td tag
    output.RenderEndTag            //closes the Tr tag
    output.RenderEndTag            //closes the Table tag
}
```

**Listing 8.1:** Creating an HTML Table Using Stack-Based HtmlTextWriter Methods.

The code in Listing 8.1 creates a very simple table containing one row with two cells, and shows the stack-based nature of the tags. The **HtmlTextWriter** tracks what tags have been "pushed" on to the stack (**AddAttribute** and **RenderBeginTag**) and therefore knows which end tag to "pop off" the stack each time the **RenderEndTag** method is called.

# Using Child Controls

HTML controls and server controls can create their own HTML. When these controls are added to a Web Part to help create HTML, they are known as *child controls*. Child controls provide the following benefits:

► HTML and Server controls can render their own markup.

► Server controls can be bound to a specific data source.

► Server controls can participate in server-side events.

Web Parts can contain child controls that exist in the **System.Web. UI.HtmlControls** or **System.Web.UI.WebControls** namespaces. Common HTML controls that may be used as child controls for Web Parts include:

► **HtmlAnchor** – Allows access to an anchor (**<A>**)tag.

► **HtmlButton** – Allows access to a button (**<button>**) tag.

► **HtmlTable** – Allows access to a table (**<table>**) tag.

► **HtmlTableCell** – Allows access to table cell (**<td>**) and table heading (**<th>**) tags.

► **HtmlTableRow** – Allows access to a table row (**<tr>**)tag.

► **HtmlTextArea** – Allows access to a text area (**<textarea>**) tag.

Common Server controls that may be used as child controls for Web Parts include:

► **DropDownList** – Displays a dropdown list on a page.

► **HyperLink** – Displays a link on a page.

► **Image** – Displays an image on a page.

► **Label** – Displays text on a page.

► **Table** – Displays a table on a page.

► **TextBox** – Displays a text box on a page.

The details of HTML and server controls are beyond the scope of this book, but you should know that HTML controls mimic the set of HTML tags, while Server controls are a rich set of controls that provide a set of properties and methods for programmers to use at the server level.

Like any other control, child controls must be declared and created. The Web Part's base class of **System.Web.UI.Control** helps with this by providing the virtual **CreateChildControl** and **EnsureChildControl** methods. The overridden **CreateChildControl** method is where the Web Part should create any child controls. Before the Web Part uses any child controls, it should call the **WebPart** class's **EnsureChildControl** method, which will in turn call **CreateChildControl** if this method has not already been called. Once the child controls are created, their properties can be modified and they can bind to data sources, participate in events, and render using the **RenderControl** method.

A Web Part using child controls should include the **INamingContainer** interface, which ensures that controls have a unique ID when rendered to the output buffer. It is not necessary to implement any methods on this interface. This is a *marker interface*, which means that it does not define any methods. It is important to include this interface when implementing child controls, in case the same Web Part is placed more than once on a Web Part page.

### *Caution:*

To avoid scripting errors on the client, it is important that content emitted for a Web Part (including any client-side script) is unique to an instance of a Web Part. This is true even if the same Web Part is placed on the same page more than once. To do this, the Web Part class provides the Qualifier property, which is guaranteed to be unique. In addition, a set of special tokens (such as _WPQ_) have been defined to allow them to be replaced in some property values with the Web Part class's **ReplaceToken** method. Refer to the SDK for more information on the **ReplaceToken** method.

Use these steps to implement a Web Part with a child control:

1　Create a new Visual C# Web Part template project in Visual Studio .NET.

2　Declare the **INamingContainer** interface.

**SYNTAX**
```
public class <WebPart Name> : Microsoft.SharePoint.
      WebPartPages.WebPart, INamingContainer
```

**EXAMPLE**
```
public class WebPartLifeCycle : Microsoft.SharePoint.
      WebPartPages.WebPart, INamingContainer
```

3　Declare all child control variables in the Web Part class.

**SYNTAX**
```
<variable type> <variable name>;
```

**EXAMPLE**
```
System.Web.UI.TextBox  txtMessage;
```

4　Override the **CreateChildControls** method. Dimension all child controls, set any child control properties, and bind any event handlers. Add the child controls to the **Controls** collection of the **System.Web.UI.Control** object. The **CreateChildControls** method must be called by the Web Part infrastructure before any child controls can be accessed.

For example, dimension a **System.Web.UI.WebControls.TextBox** named **txtMessage**. Modify the TextBox's **Text** property by adding some text, such as:

```
This message brought to you by a child control!
```

5　Add the control to the Web Part's **Controls** collection, like this:

```
protected override void CreateChildControls()
{
  base.CreateChildControls();
```

```
txtMessage = new TextBox();
txtMessage.Text =
   "This message brought to you by a child control!";
Controls.Add(txtMessage);
}
```

6   Call the Web Part's **EnsureChildControls** method before the Web Part code uses the child controls. This will ensure that the controls are created and ready to be used.

7   Call the child control's **RenderControl** method and pass in the RenderWebPart's **HtmlTextWriter** object, like this:

```
protected override void RenderWebPart(HtmlTextWriter output)
{
   output.Write(Message);
   EnsureChildControls();
   txtMessage.RenderControl(output);
}
```

The control will render itself as HTML to the output buffer

*Tech Tip:*

To create high performance Web Parts, the Web Part base class provides two mechanisms: the Part Cache and Asynchronous Fetches. With the Part Cache, the HTML (or any other data) from a previous rendering of a Web Part can be stashed away for use by future rendering. The Part Cache differs from the standard ASP.NET caching mechanisms in that it can be stored in the SharePoint database. The Part Cache is accessed through the **PartCacheRead** and **PartCacheWrite** methods. For advanced performance tuning when obtaining data from an external source, the Web Part infrastructure supports asynchronous data fetches on a separate thread, through the **RegisterWorkItem**, **GetData**, and **GetRequiresData** methods. See the SDK documentation for details on these mechanisms.

# Chapter 9

# Personalization and Web Parts

SharePoint Technologies allow a wide range of personalization options for tailoring Web Part pages and Web Parts to display information that is targeted to specific users. In this chapter, we will look at the following ways of configuring Web Parts for personalization:

► Create custom properties that use the **WebPartStorage** attribute.

► Tailor Web Part output based on the logged-in user, the **Profile** database, or Audience membership.

*Caution:*

The ability to tailor Web Part output according to the **Profile** database and audiences membership is only available to SPS. This functionality is not supported in WSS.

# Using Custom Properties to Personalize Web Parts

Users can change the content in a Web Part's frame by changing the Web Part's properties. These changes will appear to occur at runtime, since they can be done from the user's web browser interface. The user's ability to make these changes is determined by specific property attributes. An *attribute* is metadata associated with an object that can alter the handling of that object. All Web Part properties have an attribute named **WebPartStorage** that determines if the property is saved and if so, whether it is saved on a per-user or shared basis. Specifying the **WebPartStorage** attribute on a per-user basis allows a single Web Part to store the value of the property for each user, rather than for all users in the system. Declaring per-user properties on a Web Part is an effective way to enable personalization.

*Tech Tip:*

The fully qualified name for the **WebPartStorage** attribute is **Microsoft. SharePoint.WebPartPages.WebPartStorageAttribute**. It is fine to use either **WebPartStorageAttribute** or **WebPartStorage**. The .NET compiler understands either syntax.

The **WebPartStorage** attribute resides in the **Microsoft.SharePoint. WebPartPages** namespace. It contains the **Storage** enumeration, which is used to tell the XML serializer if the property should be serialized and how to store the property. The **Storage** enumeration has three values:

▶ **None** — The property is not serialized.

▶ **Shared** — The property is serialized and stored for all users of a Web Part instance.

▶ **Personal** — The property is serialized and can be stored for a particular user of a Web Part instance.

Developers are responsible for declaring the **WebPartStorage** attribute for each property according to the need of the Web Part. Certain properties may need only shared serialization. An example of such a property would be a data source connection to a Microsoft SQL Server. Other properties might benefit from a personalized serialization, such as a **Region** property used in a sales forecast Web Part, which would allow each salesperson to personalize the region that he or she focuses on.

Properties that are inherited from the **Microsoft.SharePoint.WebPartPages. WebPart** class already have their **WebPartStorage** attribute declared. For example, the **Title** property of the **WebPart** class has a **WebPartStorage** attribute set to WebPartStorage.Personal. This means that the title of a Web Part can be set on an individual basis.

When the Web Part infrastructure instantiates a Web Part class on the server, the infrastructure sets the value for each property, based on the value of the **WebPartStorage** attribute of that property. To understand how the Web Part infrastructure stores and retrieves property values, it helps to understand the serialization process of the Web Part, as described in Chapter 3. In the serialization process, a Web Part is added to a Web Part page's Web Part zone. Configuration information from the definition file (.dwp) is inserted into the database. The inserted Web Part has a single row in the database containing an associated pair of shared and default personal properties. If a user has personalized a Web Part, there is a separate set of personal properties created in a separate table. All users will use the shared properties. Users who have not personalized the Web Part will use the default personal properties. Users who have personalized the Web Part will use their specific personal properties. The Web Part infrastructure will use the correct set of personal properties for each user automatically. Figure 9.1 shows a simple flow chart for retrieving properties.

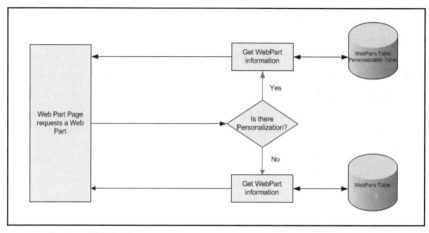

**Figure 9.1:** Retrieving Web Part Properties.

Figures 9.2, 9.3 and 9.4 show the **Site Navigator** Web Part for three different users. The Web Part has been configured by the site administrator to have a **Title** of `Site Navigator`, which is attributed as **WebPartStorage.Personal**, and a **Show_Events** value of `True`, which is attributed as **WebPartStorage.Shared**. Users with privileges to personalize Web Parts will be able to modify the **Title** property. Only users with permissions to modify the Shared View will be able to modify the **Show_Events** property and all users will receive the same shared value. The users in Figures 9.2 and 9.3 are contributors to the site. They have changed the **Title** property for their view of the Web Part. The user in Figure 9.4 is a reader who does not have the privilege to modify the Web Part and therefore receives the default properties. Notice that all three figures display the event information because it is a shared property.

> *Note:*
>
> For this chapter, the sample Site Navigator Web Part has been modified to display the current user to help clarify Figures 9.2, 9.3, and 9.4. The modified code is available online when you register this book at www.rationalpress.com.

**Darrin's Site Navigator** ▼

**User:** WSS1
\darrin_contributor

Ben's Cement
Company Project

Betsy's Equine
Center SPS Project

Darrins Health
System WSS
Project

Meg's Horse Farm
Project

SharePoint Tech
Research Center

OnInit - Control is initializing
OnLoad - Control is loading into page
CreateChildControls
OnPreRender - Control is ready to start
rendering
RenderWebPart - Creating the output

**Figure 9.2:** Darrin_Contributor with Modified Title.

**Ben's Site Navigator** ▼

**User:** WSS1
\ben_contributor

Ben's Cement
Company Project

Betsy's Equine Center
SPS Project

Darrins Health
System WSS Project

Meg's Horse Farm
Project

SharePoint Tech
Research Center

OnInit - Control is initializing
OnLoad - Control is loading into page
CreateChildControls
OnPreRender - Control is ready to start
rendering
RenderWebPart - Creating the output

**Figure 9.3:** Ben_Contributor with Modified Title.

**Site Navigator**

**User:** WSS1
\meg_reader

Ben's Cement Company
Project

Betsy's Equine Center
SPS Project

Darrins Health System
WSS Project

Meg's Horse Farm
Project

SharePoint Tech
Research Center

OnInit - Control is initializing
OnLoad - Control is loading into page
CreateChildControls
OnPreRender - Control is ready to start
rendering
RenderWebPart - Creating the output

**Figure 9.4:** Meg_Reader with Default Title.

*Note:*

**Users with privileges to add and modify pages (such as administrators and web designers) have the ability to modify the Shared View, which will affect all users who view the page. Users with the privileges to modify the Shared View should make sure they are modifying the appropriate view (either Shared or Personal). For further information on Shared and Personal Views, see Chapter 2.**

Unlike static ASP .NET server controls (where the properties are set in the `.aspx` page), dynamic Web Parts need a way to tell the system that their properties have been changed and therefore need to be saved. This is done through the **SaveProperties** property on the Web Part base class. This property starts each page render with a value of `false`. It is the responsibility of the Web Part developer to set it to `true` if any property's value changes and that change needs to be saved. If this property is not set before the Web Part's **UnLoad** event is finished executing, no changes to the properties will be persisted and any changed values will be lost.

Web Parts use the .NET XML serializer mechanism to store property values. This mechanism allows the use of the **DefaultValue** attribute and the **ShouldSerialize<name>** methods (where **<name>** is the name of the property) for determining whether a property has deviated from its default value and therefore needs to be stored. A Web Part developer should use these methods to store only properties that have changed from their default value, thus reducing the amount of space used in the SharePoint database. Overridable **ShouldSerialize** methods are included on the Web Part base class for base class properties.

# Using Tailored Web Part Output

You can tailor Web Part output to render a Web Part according to known information about the current user, which can be determined in multiple ways.

▶  Tailor output according to the current user

▶  Tailor output according to the **Profile** database

▶  Tailor output according to audience membership

## Tailor Output According to the Current User

Knowing the current user is really the starting point for tailoring the output or functionality of a Web Part. This is how property personalization works. SharePoint knows the current user and can select the appropriate property values for a Web Part. There is more than one way to determine the current user. In this section, we will look at the WSS APIs for determining the current user. The option of tailoring output according to the current user is available to both WSS and SPS.

**Site Navigator** is an example of a Web Part that is tailored to a current user. The **Site Navigator** example in Chapter 5 renders its content and available sites based on the current, logged-on user. WSS determines the list of sites to render according to the current user's security credentials available in the site's **Context** object as a part of the call to the **GetSubwebsForCurrentUser** method. In the example in Chapter 5, the content was 'tailored' because the WSS APIs returned sites based on the current, logged-on user. The **Site Navigator** Web Part for this chapter modifies the output by displaying the logged-on user. Both examples use different techniques, but the result is the same: the Web Part is personalized according to the logged-on user.

The WSS Object Model is available to both WSS and SPS. It provides the functionality to retrieve the current user credentials from ASP .NET. The **Site Navigator** Web Part example in this chapter uses the WSS Object Model to determine the current user. Once the Web Part knows who the user is, the Web Part developer is free to alter the content or functionality as appropriate to that user. The **Site Navigator** Web Part does this by rendering the user's name. This is a very simple example of tailoring the content to the user. Once the user is known, the execution path can change and additional, more specific processing can happen. Listing 9.1 shows the code for determining current users.

```
private string GetLoggedOnUser()
{
    Microsoft.SharePoint.SPWeb web;
    web = Microsoft.SharePoint.WebControls.SPControl.
        GetContextWeb(this.Context);
    return web.CurrentUser.LoginName;
}
```

**Listing 9.1:** Retrieving the Current User of a WSS or SPS Site.

**CurrentUser** is a property of the **SPWeb** object located in the **Microsoft. SharePoint** namespace. This object is available in both WSS and SPS. The code in Listing 9.1 uses a shared object called **SPControl** to retrieve the *context web*, which is the web site that the instance of the Web Part is running in. The **SPControl** object is located in the **Microsoft.SharePoint.WebControl** namepspace. Once the Web Part has an **SPWeb** object that is bound to the context web, the Web Part can easily access the current user's **LoginName** property from the **CurrentUser** property of the **SPWeb** object. The code in Listing 9.1 is actually WSS API code and is not specific to the Web Part infrastructure. Once the Web Part code has the current user's identification data, the developer can create code to alter the Web Part's content or functionality according to the user. In Listing 9.1, the **LoginName** property outputs the logged-on user's name as content, so that we can differentiate the user's view of the Web Part. A Web Part developer can easily create an execution path that is different for each user.

## Tailor Output According to the Profile Database

SharePoint Portal Server includes a **Profile** database, which contains information about each Portal user and may be populated from a directory service import, such as Microsoft Active Directory. The **Profile** database may be supplemented by user-supplied values. This profile information can be made available to Web Parts to tailor output.

The default **Profile** database contains fields such as **Account Name**, **First Name**, **Last Name**, as well as fields for addresses and phone numbers. It also contains the URL to the user's personal site. It is simple to modify the **Profile** database to add a custom field and populate it from another data source. An example could be a **Sales Territory** field, or even a key field to identify the user to an individual row in a specific database. These are not typical fields in Microsoft Active Directory, but they might be useful to a personalized Web Part.

Many system administrators are cautious about extending the Microsoft Active Directory schema. The **Profile** database resides inside SQL Server and has the default name **<site name>_PROF**. The database can be extended without fear of manipulating Active Directory. You should understand that adding or changing fields in the **Profile** database does not update the Active Directory. There is no built-in mechanism to for updating Active Directory from the **Profile** database.

Any default field or custom field is available to a Web Part using the SPS APIs. Listing 9.2 demonstrates the use of the SPS API to return the current user.

**Caution:**

The Profile database is only available with SPS. Users must have SPS installed to access the Profile database to run the code in Listing 9.2. A WSS Site will not have the available Object Model functions or the Profile database for this example.

```
private string GetLoggedOnUser()
{
    Microsoft.SharePoint.Portal.UserProfiles.ProfileLoader
        ➲ loader = Microsoft.SharePoint.Portal.UserProfiles.
        ➲ ProfileLoader.GetProfileLoader();

    Microsoft.SharePoint.Portal.UserProfiles.UserProfile prof =
        ➲ loader.GetUserProfile();

    return prof["AccountName"].ToString();
}
```

**Listing 9.2:** Current User using User Profile.

The code in Listing 9.2 is simple but powerful. First, the function creates the **ProfileLoader** object using the shared function **GetProfileLoader** of the **ProfileLoader** class. The **ProfileLoader** object will load the current user's profile from the **Profile** database into a **UserProfile** object. The **UserProfile** object contains an array of all the properties from the **Profile** database and is available using the indexer or **Item** property. **GetLoggedOnUser** returns the item for **AccountName**. Once a **UserProfile** is loaded, the Web Part can access any item in the **Profile** database.

Listing 9.3 shows the **RenderWebPart** method for the **ProfileViewer** Web Part. This simple Web Part code retrieves the user's profile information in the **UserProfile** object and displays it in a table.

```
protected override void RenderWebPart(HtmlTextWriter output)
{
    output.AddAttribute ("width", "90%");
    output.RenderBeginTag(HtmlTextWriterTag.Table);
    output.RenderBeginTag(HtmlTextWriterTag.Tr);
    output.RenderBeginTag (HtmlTextWriterTag.Td);
    output.RenderBeginTag(HtmlTextWriterTag.B);
    output.Write("Account Name:");
    output.RenderEndTag();
    output.RenderEndTag();          //close td
    output.RenderBeginTag(HtmlTextWriterTag.Td);
    //Description of site
    output.Write(GetProfileInfo("AccountName"));
    output.RenderEndTag();          //close td
    output.RenderEndTag();          //close tr
    // .........
    output.RenderBeginTag(HtmlTextWriterTag.Tr);
    output.RenderBeginTag (HtmlTextWriterTag.Td);
    output.RenderBeginTag(HtmlTextWriterTag.B);
    output.Write("Department:");
    output.RenderEndTag();
    output.RenderEndTag();          //close td
    output.RenderBeginTag(HtmlTextWriterTag.Td);
    output.Write(GetProfileInfo("Department"));
    output.RenderEndTag();          //close td
    output.RenderEndTag();          //close tr
    output.RenderEndTag();          //close table
}
private string GetProfileInfo(string ProfileField)
{
    try
    {
        Microsoft.SharePoint.Portal.UserProfiles.ProfileLoader
            ➲ loader = Microsoft.SharePoint.Portal.UserProfiles.
            ➲ ProfileLoader.GetProfileLoader();
```

```
Microsoft.SharePoint.Portal.UserProfiles.UserProfile prof =
    ➲ loader.GetUserProfile();

    return prof[ProfileField].ToString();
}
catch(Exception Ex)
{
    return "";
}
}
```

**Listing 9.3:** Profile Viewer RenderWebPart Method.

**FREE**

*Bonus:*

The full Profile Viewer code is available online when you register this book at
www.rationalpress.com.

## Tailor Output According to the Audience Membership

Determining membership in an audience is another option for tailoring content to the specific users. *Audiences* are used by SPS to target information to a group of users. Audiences are *not* a security group; in fact, they have nothing to do with security. They are simply a mechanism to group users from multiple sources, such as security and distribution groups. Audiences can also be created from queries against the **Profile** database. Audiences are created and maintained by choosing **Site Settings** ⇨ **Manage Audiences**. Audience membership can be used to personalize Web Parts for a group of users.

Because audiences are comprised of zero or more users, the personalization provided with audiences is targeted to a group, not just to the current user. The SPS APIs provide an **AudienceManager** object that will determine if a user is a member of an audience. The code in Listing 9.4 creates the **AudienceManager** object and checks to see if the current user is a member of the audience named in the **AudienceNames** parameter.

```
private bool InAudience( string AudienceName)
{
    try
    {
        Microsoft.SharePoint.Portal.Audience.AudienceManager audMgr =
        ➲ new Microsoft.SharePoint.Portal.Audience.AudienceManager();

        return
        audMgr.IsMemberOfAudience(GetProfileInfo("AccountName"),
        ➲ AudienceName);
    }
    catch(Exception  Ex)
    {
        return false;
    }
}
```

**Listing 9.4:** Determining Audience Membership.

The **InAudience** method simply creates an **AudienceManger** object and calls the **IsMemberOfAudience** method. The **IsMemberOfAudience** method accepts a user's account name and the audience name. For this example, the code is using the helper function we created for the **UserProfile** example to determine the user's account name.

✎ *Note:*

**Audiences are compiled by SPS. The process of compiling an audience creates a membership listing for the audience based on the rules of the audience. If the expected membership in the audience does not appear to be correct, you may need to recompile the audience.**

Figure 9.5 shows the **TeamLeads** audience, which is comprised of users with the **Title** of **TeamLeads** and users who exist in the administrator group. If users meet one or both of these conditions, they will be included as members.

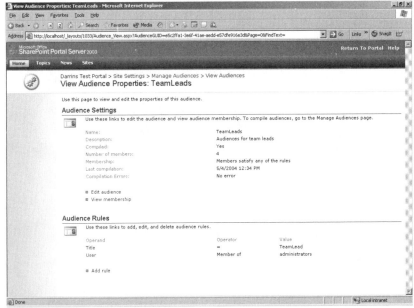

**Figure 9.5:** Properties of the TeamLeads Audience.

The **AudienceDemo** Web Part in Figures 9.6, 9.7, and 9.8 tailors the content according to audience membership. If the current user is in the **TeamLeads** audience, the Web Part will display a list of audiences associated with the current site, as well as the membership of those audiences. If the current user is a member of the **Boss** audience, the Web Part will render a list of users that report to the current user. If the current user is not a member of either audience, a simple message is displayed.

**Figure 9.6:** Audience Demo – No Membership.

**Figure 9.8:** Audience Demo – Member of Boss Audience.

**Figure 9.7:** Audience Demo – Member of TeamLeads Audience.

# Did you know?

Did you know that Web Parts on SharePoint Portal Pages can be targeted to an audience?

A user can use the tool pane to select one or more target audiences. If the user belongs to at least one of the targeted audiences, he or she will see the Web Part.

# Chapter 10

# Connectable Web Parts

Connectable Web Parts are Web Parts that exchange information and alter their content or functionality accordingly. Since the first version of Web Parts hosted by SharePoint Portal Server 2001, developers have been able to create Web Parts that effectively communicate information between each other.

SharePoint Portal Server 2001 utilized the Digital Dashboard Service Component (DDSC) to facilitate connections between Web Parts. Using this component to connect Web Parts required each Web Part to know and understand each Web Part it wanted to communicate with. Each Web Part was required to register the events it fired and the events it wanted to receive. Web Parts can still utilize the same basic technique that the DDSC provided in SPS 2001 by using the Web Part Page Services Component (WPSC) for client site connections, though the WPSC is now implemented in JavaScript instead of the ActiveX implementation used by the DDSC.

The latest version of Web Parts can now utilize a server-side connection via standard, connectable interfaces, as well as client-side connections via a JavaScript implementation. A connectable interface is a set of methods used by the Web Part infrastructure to enable information to pass between Web Parts. There are many benefits to using these standard interfaces instead of the older approach. Each Web Part that implements connectable interfaces is free to connect to Web Parts that implement the reciprocal interface; the Web Parts do not require any prior knowledge of each other. Another benefit of this standard interface architecture is that connections can now be made by end users and page authors, in addition to developers and administrators.

In this chapter, we will look at the connection interfaces and how they work to create connectable Web Parts. We will create a new Web Part that will connect to a modified version of the **Site Navigator** Web Part used in previous chapters. The new Web Part, called **Site Selector**, will implement the **ICellProvider** interface and the **Site Navigator** Web Part will implement the **ICellConsumer** interface. In this chapter, we will be looking at server-side connections only.

## *Connectable Interfaces*

Web Parts that implement at least one of the connectable interfaces can participate in connections. Connectable Web Parts can implement *provider* and *consumer* interfaces. As their names imply, providers send information, while consumers receive it. There are six available provider/consumer interface pairs:

▶ **ICellProvider/ICellConsumer** — Provides/Consumes a single value.

▶ **IRowProvider/IRowConsumer** — Provides/Consumes a single row of information.

▶ **IListProvider/IListConsumer** — Provides/Consumes a list of data.

▶ **IFilterProvider/IFilterConsumer** — Provides/Consumes a filter expression of one or more columns and values.

▶ **IParametersOutProvider/IParametersOutConsumer** — Provides a list of parameters to the consumer.

▶ **IParametersInProvider/IParametersInConsumer** — Provides a list of parameters that the consumer can receive from the provider.

**Note:**

Connections using the **IParametersInConsumer** interface must be made with Front Page 2003 or another SPS/WSS-aware HTML editor.

A Web Part that implements a consumer interface can connect to one or more Web Parts that implement the corresponding provider interface. An example would be a Web Part that implements the **ICellConsumer** interface and connects to a Web Part that implements the corresponding **ICellProvider** interface. In this example, the consumer is expecting a single value and the provider is providing the single value. Some of the Web Parts that are installed with WSS and SPS implement connectable interfaces. For example, a ListView Web Part that is used to display lists in a Web Part can provide a cell to an Image Web Part. A ListView Web Part can also consume a filter from another Web Part and filter its list. In instances where a Web Part does not implement the correct corresponding interface, Web Parts can take advantage of built-in interface transformers provided by the Web Part infrastructure when connections are being created by the user.

There are four available transformers:

- ▶ IRowProvider — ICellConsumer

- ▶ IRowProvider — IFilterConsumer

- ▶ IParametersOutProvider — IParametersInConsumer

- ▶ IRowProvider — IParametersInConsumer

All of the necessary classes and interface definitions for building connectable Web Parts are located in the **Microsoft.SharePoint.WebPartPages. Communication** namespace. If you plan to develop connectable Web Parts, you should understand the various classes included in this namespace. Information about the Communication namespace can be found in the SharePoint Products and Technologies SDK on the Microsoft web site at `http://www.microsoft.com/ downloads/details.aspx?familyid=1c64af62-c2e9-4ca3-a2a0-7d4319980011&dis playlang=en`.

## *Connections Cycle*

Most of the methods used to implement the connection are virtual methods of the **Microsoft.SharePoint.WebPartPages.WebPart** class. These overidden methods will call the methods specific to the implemented interface. The six types of connection interfaces are quite similar. Let's look at the **ICellProvider/ ICellConsumer** connection cycle as an example.

Figure 10.1 depicts the execution of methods between the Web Part infrastructure and two Web Parts.

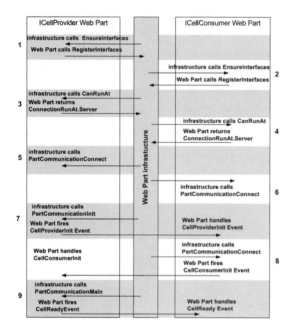

**Figure 10.1:** Connection Cycle for Connected Web Parts.

In Figure 10.1, the **ICellProvider** Web Part is on the left; the **ICellConsumer** Web Part is on the right. The Web Part infrastructure is in the middle. All of the depicted calls occur during the **PreRender** phase of the Web Part. The **OnPreRender** event of each Web Part is fired and handled after the connection has been created.

Figure 10.1 shows the steps specific to creating a Web Part connection in the **PreRender** phase of the Web Part:

1. The Web Part infrastructure calls the provider Web Part's **EnsureInterfaces** method. The provider Web Part responds by calling its **RegisterInterfaces** method, which provides the Web Part infrastructure with the following data:

   - A friendly name

- Interface type

- The maximum number of connections allowed

- The location where the connection can run

- The object that implements the interface

- A client-side name (if the connection can run on the client side)

- The menu ToolTip description

2. The Web Part infrastructure calls the consumer Web Part's **EnsureInterfaces** method. The consumer Web Part responds by calling its **RegisterInterfaces** method.

3. The Web Part infrastructure calls the provider Web Part's **CanRunAt** method. The provider Web Part responds with a value from the **ConnectionRunAt** enumeration, which can be `Client`, `None`, `Server`, or `ServerAndClient`.

4. The Web Part infrastructure calls the consumer Web Part's **CanRunAt** method. The consumer Web Part responds with a value from the **ConnectionRunAt** enumeration, which can be `Client`, `None`, `Server`, or `ServerAndClient`.

5. The Web Part infrastructure calls the consumer Web Part's **PartCommunicationConnect** method, which lets the Web Part know that it has a new connection. This method passes the following data as parameters:

- The **WebPart** object that will be connected

- The interface type and names

- The location where the connection will run, which can be Server or Client

6. The Web Part infrastructure calls the consumer Web Part's **PartCommunicationConnect** method, which lets the Web Part know that it has a new connection.

7.   The Web Part infrastructure calls the provider Web
     Part's **PartCommunicationInit** method, which gives the
     provider Web Part a chance to initialize its communication
     interface. This function should create and initialize the
     **<provider>InitEventArgs** and fire the proper init event defined
     by the implemented interface, such as **CellProviderInit** or
     **RowProviderInit**. The consumer Web Part must handle the event.
     This event allows the provider Web Part to notify the consumer
     Web Part about the information to be exchanged, such as the
     schema of the data to be provided in the connection. The consumer
     Web Part has the option to tailor the output or functionality based
     on the received information. The **PartCommunicationInit** method
     is only called if a connection exists.

8.   The Web Part infrastructure calls the consumer Web
     Part's **PartCommunicationInit** method, which gives the
     consumer Web Part a chance to initialize its communication
     interface. This function should create and initialize the
     **<provider>InitEventArgs** and fire the proper init event defined
     by the implemented interface, such as **CellConsumerInit**. The
     provider Web Part must handle the event. This event allows the
     consumer Web Part to notify the provider Web Part about the
     information to be exchanged. For example, the consumer may pass
     a filter criteria to the provider so that the provider can filter the data
     to be sent. The **PartCommunicationInit** method is only called if a
     connection exists.

9.   The Web Part infrastructure calls the provider Web Part's
     **PartCommunicationMain** method. The provider Web Part should
     fire the appropriate **<interface>Ready** event, such as **CellReady**
     or **RowReady**. The provider Web Part will pass the information
     using the **<interface>ReadyEventArgs (CellReadyEventArgs**
     or **RowReadyArgs)**. The consumer Web Part handles the
     **<interface>Ready Event** and receives information from the
     **<interface>ReadyEventArgs**.

## *Implementing the ICellProvider Interface*

The **ICellProvider** interface is used to provide a single value to a connected Web Part. To demonstrate an **ICellProvider** interface implementation, we will create a **Site Selector** Web Part that will implement the **ICellProvider** interface and provide a URL to a connected Web Part. Refer to Chapter 5 for details on creating a Web Part.

To implement an **ICellProvider** interface for a Connectable Web Part:

1. Open an existing Web Part project in Visual Studio .NET by selecting **File ⇨ Open ⇨ Project**. For example, select an existing **RationalPressWebParts** project that contains the **Site Navigator** Web Part.

2. Add a new provider Web Part class. Right-click the solution name in the Visual Studio .NET **Solution Explorer** pane and select **Add New Item** from the pop-up menu. Select **Provider Web Part**, provide a name, and click the **Open** button. This example adds a new provider Web Part named **Provider.cs**.

3. Provide a meaningful name for the Web Part named **ProviderWebPart1**, located in the new provider **WebPart** class. In this example, the **WebPart** class is renamed **SiteSelector**.

4. Modify the class-level **XmlRoot** attribute. Refer to Chapter 4 for information about modifying class-level attributes.

5. Modify the namespace, if desired. Our example changes the namespace to **RationalPress.WebParts**.

6. Add to the class any controls that will be used. In our example, the **Site Selector** Web Part has a single dropdown list control.

| SYNTAX |
| --- |

```
<scope> <type> <name>
```

| EXAMPLE |
| --- |

```
private System.Web.UI.WebControls.DropDownList dlSites;
```

7. Modfiy the **cellName** value. The **cellName** is a class-level property that is passed to the connected Web Part. In our example, the **cellName** property of the **Site Selector** Web Part is set to Site URL.

8. Override the **CreateChildControls** method. See Chapter 8 for information on the **CreateChildControls** method. Listing 10.1 shows the **CreateChildControls** method for our **Site Selector** Web Part.

```
protected override void CreateChildControls()
{
        base.CreateChildControls ();
        dlSites = new System.Web.UI.WebControls.DropDownList();
        dlSites.AutoPostBack = true;
        Controls.Add(dlSites);
}
```

**Listing 10.1:** CreateChildControls Method of the Site Selector Web Part.

9. Modify the **OnPreRender** method, which is called just prior to the rendering of the Web Part. Listing 10.2 shows the **OnPreRender** method for the **Site Selector** Web Part. If you are following this example, make sure to replace the **<Your Site Title>** and **<Your Site URL>** variables with valid information for your sites.

```
protected override void OnPreRender(EventArgs e)
{
        base.OnPreRender (e);
        if(!this.Page.IsPostBack || dlSites.Items.Count <1)
        {
                dlSites.Items.Add(new ListItem
                    ➲ ("<Your SiteTitle>","<Your Site URL>"));
        ...}
}
```

**Listing 10.2:** OnPreRender Method of the Site Selector Web Part.

10. Modify the **RenderWebPart** method. Refer to Chapter 4 if you need to review the **RenderWebPart** method. This example's **RenderWebPart** method is shown in Listing 10.3.

```
protected override void RenderWebPart(HtmlTextWriter output)
{
        dlSites.RenderControl(output);
}
```

**Listing 10.3:** RenderWebPart Method of the Site Selector Web Part.

The **Provider Web Part** template includes all of the required **ICellProvider** methods. For a simple connectable Web Part, only the **PartCommunicationMain** method requires our attention. See the "Connection Cycle" section of this chapter for information on the methods used by a connectable Web Part.

11. Modify the **PartCommunicationMain** method to pass the cell value to the connected Web Part.

**SYNTAX**

```
public override void PartCommunicationMain()
{
        if (CellReady != null)
        {
                CellReadyEventArgs cellReadyArgs = new
                        ➲ CellReadyEventArgs();
                cellReadyArgs.Cell = <value to pass>;
                CellReady(this, cellReadyArgs);
        }
}
```

**EXAMPLE**

```
public override void PartCommunicationMain()
{
        if (CellReady != null)
        {
                CellReadyEventArgs cellReadyArgs = new
                        ➲ CellReadyEventArgs();
                cellReadyArgs.Cell =dlSites.SelectedValue;
                CellReady(this, cellReadyArgs);
        }
}
```

12. Add a definition file to the project. Refer to Chapter 5 for an example of adding and modifying a definition file. For this example, a definition file is added and named SiteSelector.dwp.

13. Make sure the Web Part is safe to render. Refer to Chapter 4 to review how to mark a Web Part as safe to render.

14. Import the definition file and add the Web Part to a site's web page.

Figure 10.2 shows the **Site Selector** Web Part.

**Figure 10.2:** Site Selector Web Part.

## *Implementing the ICellConsumer Interface*

The **ICellConsumer** interface is used to consume a single value from a connected Web Part. To demonstrate an **ICellConsumer** interface implementation, we will create a new **Site Navigator** Web Part that will implement the **ICellConsumer** interface.

The **Site Navigator** Web Part displays any subsites of the current site that the current user is allowed to see. We will modify the **Site Navigator** Web Part to accept a starting URL. If the starting URL is available, the **Site Navigator** Web Part will list the available subsites for the starting URL. If there is no starting URL available, **Site Navigator** will display the subsites for the current site.

To implement an **ICellConsumer** interface for a Connectable Web Part:

1. Open an existing Web Part project in Visual Studio .NET by selecting **File ⇨ Open ⇨ Project**. Our example selects an existing **RationalPressWebParts** project that contains the **Site Navigator** Web Part and the **Site Selector** Web Part.

2. Add a new consumer **WebPart** class. Right-click the solution name in the Visual Studio .NET **Solution Explorer** pane, and select **Add New Item** from the pop-up menu. Select **Consumer Web Part**, provide a name, and click the **Open** button. This example adds a new provider Web Part named **Consumer.cs**.

3. Provide a meaningful name for the Web Part named **ConsumerWebPart1**, located in the new consumer WebPart class. In our example, the name of the **WebPart** class is changed to **SiteNavConsumer**.

4. Modify the class-level **XmlRoot** attribute. See Chapter 4 for information about class-level attributes.

5. Modify the namespace, if desired. Our example modifies the namespace to **RationalPress.WebParts**.

6. Modify the value of the **cellName** property, which is a class-level property that is passed to the connected Web Part. The **cellName** property of the **Site Selector** Web Part is set to Site URL.

7. Modify the **WebPart** class to render content. To simplify the example, we will copy from the existing **Site Navigator** Web Part, and remove the **RenderWebPart** method in the new **Site Navigator** example. Chapter 5 shows how to create the **Site Navigator** Web Part. For this example, copy the content of the **SiteNav WebPart** class to the **SiteNavConsumer WebPart** class.

The consumer Web Part template creates all the required methods of the **ICellConsumer** interface. For a simple connectable Web Part, only the **CellReady** method requires our attention. The "Connection Cycle" section in this chapter explains each of the methods used by a connectable Web Part.

8. Modify the **CellReady** method, which is called by the provider. The single cell value that is passed to the consumer is a property of the **CellReadyEventArgs**. Access the data from the **cellReadyArgs.Cell** property. For our example, the cell value is placed in the **_SiteURL** variable, which is used to determine the starting site for the **Site Navigator** Web Part.

**SYNTAX**

```
public void CellReady(object sender,
CellReadyEventArgs
cellReadyArgs)
{
        if(cellReadyArgs.Cell != null)
        {
                <variable name> =
                  ➲ cellReadyArgs.Cell.ToString();
        }
}
```

**EXAMPLE**

```
public void CellReady(object sender,
CellReadyEventArgs cellReadyArgs)
        {
                if(cellReadyArgs.Cell != null)
                {
                        _ siteURL = cellReadyArgs.Cell.
                                ➲ ToString();
                }
        }
```

9.  Add a definition file to the project. See Chapter 5 for details
    on adding and modifying a definition file. For our example, a
    definition file is added and named `SiteNavigatorConsumer.`
    `dwp`.

10. Make sure the Web Part is safe to render. Refer to Chapter 4 to
    review how to mark a Web Part as safe to render.

11. Import the definition file and add the Web Part to a site's web page.

Figure 10.3 displays the **Site Selector** and **Site Navigator** Web Parts before
they are connected. The **Site Selector** has selected the SPS SDK site, but the
connectable **Site Navigator** is displaying the subsites for the current site rather
than the SPS SDK site. A change in the **Site Selector** Web Part will not cause a
change in the **Site Navigator** Web Part.

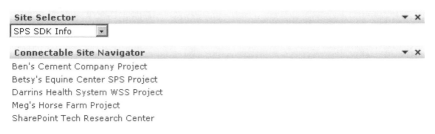

**Figure 10.3:** Two Unconnected Web Parts: Site Navigator and Site Selector.

# *Connecting the Web Parts*

In our example, the **Site Selector** Web Part implements the ICellProvider
interface and the **Site Navigator** implements the **ICellConsumer** interface. End
users can connect the Web Parts if they are located on the same page.

To connect the two Web Parts:

1.  Select the down arrow on one of the two Web Parts to access
    the Web Part menu. You can do this on either Web Part, but the
    example in Figure 10.4 shows the menu being selected from the **Site**
    **Navigator** Web Part.

2.  Select the **Modify Shared Web Part** link to place the page in design mode.

3.  From the **Web Part** menu of the Web Part you are connecting, choose **Connections Consumes a cell from**, and the Web Part to connect to. For our example, we will choose **Connections Consumes a cell from Site Selector**, as shown in Figure 10.4. The menu items will display all Web Parts that can create a connection with the selected Web Part.

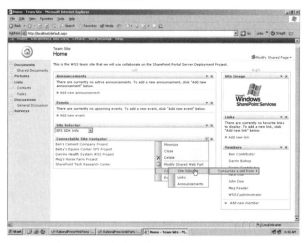

**Figure 10.4:** Connecting to the Site Selector Web Part.

Once the Web Part is selected, the Web Parts are connected. In our example, the **Site Navigator** displays the subsites for the SPS SDK site. Figure 10.5 shows the two Web Parts after the connection has been created.

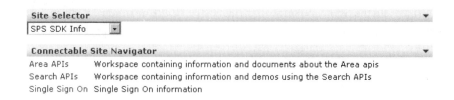

**Figure 10.5:** Two Web Parts Connected.

# Deploying Web Part Assemblies

Web Part definitions can be installed into Web Part galleries to provide a simple mechanism for users to browse and add Web Parts to Web Part pages. As discussed in Chapter 2, users can drag and drop Web Parts from galleries to a page without needing to pass definition files between users.

There are actually two locations where a Web Part assembly can be located: in the bin directory of a virtual server or in the Global Assembly Cache (GAC). In Chapters 4 and 5, we deployed a Web Part by placing its assembly in the virtual server's bin directory and importing the definition file to place an instance of the Web Part on the page. This chapter shows how to deploy Web Part assemblies to the bin directory and to the Global Assembly Cache. Deploying to the bin directory is generally quicker than deploying to the GAC, but we'll look at the pros and cons of selecting one location over the other. We will also add and delete Web Part definition files in the Site Gallery and the Virtual Server Gallery.

## *Deploying Web Part Assemblies to the Bin Directory*

The bin directory is located in the root of the virtual server. If the bin directory does not exist, you can create it as a new folder named bin at the virtual root. Keep the following issues in mind when considering whether to deploy Web Part assemblies to the bin directory:

▶ It is simple to deploy assemblies to the bin directory. Signing the assembly is not required. A strong name is not required.

▶ Trust levels are defined in the web.config file with the **trust** element. See Chapter 6 for information on Code Access Security and trust levels.

▶ Assemblies will be available only to a single virtual server.

▶ If you choose to access any external resources, the class resource for a web part in the bin directory is located at http://<servername>/wpresources/<AssemblyName>. For more information on accessing external resources, see the bonus Chapter 13, available after you register this book online at www.rationalpress.com.

If your Web Part is targeted to sites on a particular server, you should consider deploying to the bin directory. For details on how to create a Web Part and deploy the assembly to the bin directory, see Chapter 4.

# Deploying Web Part Assemblies to the Global Assembly Cache

The GAC is a single, well-known location for deploying assemblies. Keep the following issues in mind when considering whether to deploy Web Part assemblies to the GAC:

▶ You must sign the assembly and provide strong name information in the **SafeControl** element in the web.config file and in the **Assembly** element in the .dwp file. A *strong name* is the combination of **Assembly Name**, **Culture**, **Version** and **PublicKeyToken** properties of the assembly.

▶ Assemblies will be available to all virtual servers on the server.

▶ Assemblies automatically receive **Full** trust levels. See Chapter 6 for information on Code Access Security and trust levels.

▶ If you choose to access any external resources, the class resource path is located at

`http://<servername>/ _ wpresources/<AssemblyName>/<Version _ CultureInfo.CurrentUICulture.Name _ PublicKey>`. For more information on accessing external resources, see the bonus Chapter 13, available after you register this book online (see the last page in this book for more information about registration).

If you are maintaining multiple virtual servers and sites, or if all virtual servers will need the same Web Parts in the assembly, you should consider placing the assembly in the GAC.

To deploy an assembly to the GAC, the assembly must be signed with a public key and the **SafeControl** entry must be modified with a strong name. The **Assembly** element in the definition file (`.dwp`) will need also the strong name.

Deploying Web Part assemblies to the GAC requires the following procedures:

▶ Creating a public key

▶ Signing the assembly with the public key

▶ Modifying the **SafeControl** entry in the `web.config` file with a strong name

▶ Modifying the definition file (`.dwp`) with the strong name

## Creating a Public Key

In order for the assembly to be installed in the GAC, it must have a strong name. The strong name requires the **PublicKeyToken** attribute, derived from signing the assembly with a public key.

To create a public key:

1. At the command prompt, navigate to the location of the `sn.exe` tool. By default, this is located in the `\<Visual Studio>\SDK\v<version>\bin` directory.

2. Use the following syntax to create the public key using the `sn.exe` tool with the **–k** option.

**SYNTAX**

```
sn -k <filename>
```

**EXAMPLE**

```
sn -k c:\rpress.snk
```

This example will create a file at the `c:\` directory named `rpress.snk`. Figure 11.1 shows the command prompt after the file has been created.

```
C:\Program Files\Microsoft Visual Studio .NET 2003\SDK\v1.1\Bin>sn -k C:\rpress.
snk

Microsoft (R) .NET Framework Strong Name Utility  Version 1.1.4322.573
Copyright (C) Microsoft Corporation 1998-2002. All rights reserved.

Key pair written to C:\rpress.snk

C:\Program Files\Microsoft Visual Studio .NET 2003\SDK\v1.1\Bin>
```

**Figure 11.1:** Creating the Public Key File.

## Signing the Assembly with the Public Key

To sign the assembly with the public key:

1.  Copy the public key file to the project directory. For this example, copy `rpress.snk` to the `bin` directory of the virtual server.

2.  Modify the **AssemblyKeyFile** attribute located in the `Assemblyinfo.cs` file to include the location of the public key file. For our example, open the **Site Navigator** Web Part and the `Assemblyinfo.cs` file. Modify the **AssemblyKeyFile** value to look like:

    ```
    [assembly: AssemblyKeyFile("..\\..\\rpress.snk")]
    ```

3.  Set the version number of the assembly in the `Assemblyinfo.cs` file. The **AssemblyVersion** attribute should be set before the file is built. The version plays a role in identifying the assembly after it is signed.

In our example, the **AssemblyVersion** attribute appears as:

```
[assembly: AssemblyVersion("1.0.0.1")]
```

> ## Note:
>
> The default for the assembly attribute is **AssemblyVersion("1.0.\*")**. This syntax tells the compiler to increment the version for each successive build. A change to the version number will result in a change to the assembly's strong name. Any Web Part definition file that is looking for a previous version of the Web Part will not be able to locate the correct assembly file due to the changed strong name.

4. Rebuild the project to build in the public key information.

   Install the signed assembly into the GAC by using the **/i** option of the Global Assembly Cache Tool (`gacutil.exe`) from the command line. The Global Assembly Cache Tool is located in the .NET Framework path (for example, `<root>\Windows\Microsoft.Net\Framework\v1.1.4322\`). For this example, use the following command to install the **RationalPressWebParts** assembly into the GAC: `gacutil -i RationalPressWebParts.dll`. Figure 11.2 displays the GAC with the **RationalPressWebParts** assembly highlighted.

**Figure 11.2:** RationalPressWebParts Assembly Located in the GAC.

> **Note:**
>
> **The GAC is typically located in the** %systemroot%\assembly directory.
> **You can launch an Explorer pane for the GAC by choosing Run... from the**
> **Start menu and entering** %systemroot%\assembly.

5.   Remove the copy of the original assembly from the bin directory.

## Modifying the SafeControl Entry in the web.config file

The signed assembly now has a strong name, which is the combination of
**Assembly Name**, **Culture**, **Version** and **PublicKeyToken** properties. The
**PublicKeyToken** property is derived from the public key file. Since .NET will
use the strong name to identify the assembly, you must modify the name of the
assembly in the **SafeControl** entry in the web.config file.

1.   Use Notepad to navigate to the virtual server's root directory,
     usually located at c:\inetpub\wwwroot, and open the
     web.config file.

2.   Modify the **SafeControl** entry for the Web Part, according to the
     following syntax:

**SYNTAX**

```
<SafeControl Assembly="<Assembly Name>,
        Version=<version of the assembly>,
         Culture=<culture>,
         PublicKeyToken=<PublicKeyToken from Key File>"
         Namespace="<Web Part Namespace>"
         TypeName="<* or TypeName>" Safe="<True|False>" />
```

**EXAMPLE**

```
<SafeControl Assembly="RationalPressWebParts,
        Version=1.0.0.1,
         Culture=neutral,
         PublicKeyToken=14b52a278febeab7"
         Namespace="RationalPress.WebParts"
         TypeName="*" Safe="True" />
```

The example shows the **SafeControl** entry for the strong-named **Site Navigator** Web Part. The **Version, Culture,** and **PublicKeyToken** attributes are specific to your Web Part. To make your Web Part work, you must apply your Web Part's values to these attributes.

*Tech Tip:*

You can find the Public Key Token information by viewing the **Properties** dialog box of the assembly in the GAC, or by using the **Strong Name Tool** (sn. exe) with the -T option.

3.  Save the web.config file.

## Modifying the Assembly Element in the Definition File

To modify the .dwp file's **Assembly** element to reflect the strong name for the assembly:

1.  Open the .dwp file for your Web Part, and modify the **Assembly** element according to the following syntax:

SYNTAX
```
<Assembly>'Assembly Name', Version='Version',
Culture='Culture', PublicKeyToken='PublicKeyToken from Key
File'</Assembly>
```

EXAMPLE
```
<Assembly>RationalPressWebParts, Version=1.0.0.1,
Culture=neutral, PublicKeyToken=14b52a278febeab7</Assembly>
```

The example displays the **Assembly** element of the .dwp file for the **Site Navigator** Web Part. The **Version, Culture**, and **PublicKeyToken** attributes are specific to your Web Part. To make your Web Part work, you must apply your Web Part's values to these attributes.

2.  Save the .dwp file.

3.  Import the `.dwp` file and place the Web Part on the page, as described in Chapter 2.

# Adding and Deleting the Definition File in Web Part Galleries

After deploying a Web Part assembly to either the GAC or the `bin` directory, you must determine where to install the definition file to make it readily available to users and to other sites. There are three galleries where you can browse for Web Parts:

▶  Site Gallery

▶  Virtual Server Gallery

▶  Online Gallery

You can install the definition file into the Site Gallery or the Virtual Server Gallery. Maintaining and creating an Online Gallery is not covered in this book. See Chapter 2 for information about Web Part galleries.

## Adding and Deleting a Web Part Definition in a Site Gallery

Installing the definition file to the Site Gallery is fairly simple. The definition files deployed to the Site Gallery can be seen by users when they browse to the **<Site Name> Site Gallery** in the gallery tool pane. These Web Parts will also show up as the result of searches across the available galleries. Each Web Part definition installed to the Site Gallery is only available in the site collection to which it is deployed. A *site collection* is the top-level site and any subsites. A definition file can be added to multiple Site galleries.

### Deploying a Web Part Definition to a Site Gallery

The steps for deploying a Web Part definition to a Site Gallery differ slightly between WSS and SPS.

To deploy a Web Part to a WSS Site Gallery:

1.  Click the **Site Settings** link at the top of the site page. The **Site Settings** page will appear. Figure 11.3 shows the WSS link to the **Site Administration** page.

**Figure 11.3:** Link to the Site Administration Page in WSS.

2.  Select the **Go to Site Administration** link. The top-level **Site Administration** page will appear.

3.  Click the **Manage Web Part Gallery** link located under the **Site Collection Galleries** category. The **Web Part Gallery** page shows the available Web Part `.dwp` files, as seen in Figure 11.4.

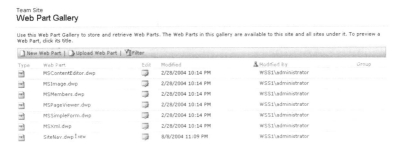

**Figure 11.4:** Web Part Gallery for the Team Web Site in WSS.

4.  Upload a Web Part `.dwp` file to the Site Gallery by clicking the **Upload Web Part** link in the title bar.

5.  In the **Upload Web Part** page, click the **Browse** button to browse to the `.dwp` file and click the **Open** button. The `.dwp` file is uploaded to the Site Gallery and is available for users to search and browse in the tool pane.

To deploy a Web Part to an SPS Site Gallery:

1.  Click the **Site Settings** link in the upper-right corner of the site page.

2.  Click the **Manage security and additional settings** link. The **Manage security and additional settings** page will appear.

3.  Click the **Manage Web Part Gallery** link located under the **Templates and Web Parts** category. The **Web Part Gallery** page shows the available Web Part .dwp files.

4.  Upload a Web Part .dwp file to the Site Gallery by clicking the **Upload Web Part** link in the title bar.

5.  In the **Upload Web Part** page, click the **Browse** button to browse to the .dwp file and click the **Open** button. The .dwp file is uploaded to the Site Gallery and is available for users to search and browse in the tool pane.

## Note:

It is important to understand that the Site Gallery contains only the Web Part definition file and not the assembly where the actual code resides. The .dwp file must point to the assembly that is already installed on the server by a server administrator. Uploading the .dwp file does not make any changes to the **SafeControl** element in the web.config file.

### Deleting a Web Part Definition from a Site Gallery

The steps for deleting a Web Part definition to a Site Gallery differ slightly between WSS and SPS.

To delete a .dwp file from a WSS Site Gallery:

1.  Click the **Site Settings** link at the top of the site page. The **Site Settings** page will appear.

2. Click the **Go to Site Administration** link. The top-level **Site Administration** page will appear.

3. In the **Site Collection Galleries** category, click the **Manage Web Part Gallery** link. The Site Gallery shows the available Web Part .dwp files.

4. Click the **Edit** icon for the row that lists the Web Part definition file to delete. The **Edit** icon for the installed definition files on the Team Site can be seen in Figure 11.4.

5. In the screen that appears, click the **Delete** link from the menu bar.

To delete a .dwp file from an SPS Site Gallery:

1. Click the **Site Settings** link in the upper-right corner of the site page.

2. Click the **Manage security and additional settings** link. The **Manage security and additional settings** page will appear.

3. Click the **Manage Web Part Gallery** link located under the **Templates and Web Parts** category. The **Web Part Gallery** page shows the available Web Part .dwp files.

4. Click the **Edit** icon for the row that lists the Web Part definition file to delete.

5. In the screen that appears, click the **Delete** link from the menu bar.

## Installing a Web Part Definition to the Virtual Server Gallery

Adding a Web Part definition file to the Virtual Server Gallery requires more steps than installing a definition to the Site Gallery. The following tasks are necessary:

▶ Modify the `Manifest.xml` file.

▶ Create the CAB file.

▶ Install the CAB file using `STSAdm.exe`.

You must modify the `Manifest.xml` file, which contains information such as the **SafeControl** entry, resources, assembly name, and the definition files to be installed. The Web Part must then be packaged into a Cabinet file (CAB) and installed using the `STSAdm.exe` command line tool. A *CAB file* is one or more compressed files and/or directories. You can use Visual Studio .NET to create a CAB file, but there are also third party tools and an SDK that can do this. The `STSAdm.exe` tool is a command line tool that can do much more than install definition files to a Virtual Server Gallery. For our purposes, we will look at only two operations for the `STSAdm.exe` tool: **addwppack** and **deletewppack**.

## Modify the Manifest.xml File

The `Manifest.xml` file should already be part of a project started with the **Web Part Library** template (see Chapter 5), so the file should only need to be modified rather than created.

To modify the `Manifest.xml` file:

1. Open the `Manifest.xml` file in Visual Studio .NET.

2. In Visual Studio .NET, open a project based on the **Web Part Library Template**. This example for this section will open the **Site Navigator** Web Part.

3. Use Visual Studio .NET to modify the `Manifest.xml` by adding any required **SafeContol** elements and .dwp files. A single `Manifest.xml` file may include information for one or more Web Parts.

Listing 11.1 displays the `Manifest.xml` file for the **Site Navigator** Web Part.

```
<?xml version="1.0"?>
<WebPartManifest
xmlns="http://schemas.microsoft.com/WebPart/v2/Manifest">
<Assemblies>
    <Assembly FileName="RationalPress.dll">
        <SafeControls>
            <SafeControl Assembly="RationalPressWebParts,
            ↪ Version=1.0.0.1, Culture=neutral,
            ↪ PublicKeyToken=14b52a278febeab7"
            ↪ Namespace="RationalPress.WebParts" TypeName="*"
            ↪ Safe="True" />
        </SafeControls>
    </Assembly>
</Assemblies>
<DwpFiles>
    <DwpFile FileName="SiteNav.dwp"/>
</DwpFiles>
</WebPartManifest>
```

**Listing 11.1:** Site Navigator Manifest.xml File.

The `Manifest.xml` file contains elements that are specific to a particular assembly. To use the `Manifest.xml` file shown in Listing 11.1 for your own assembly, you must change the **Version**, **PublicKeyToken**, **Assembly FileName**, and **Culture** attributes.

## Create the CAB File

To create a CAB file with Visual Studio .NET:

1. Add a Visual Studio .NET CAB Project to the Web Part solution. The **CAB Project** template is located in the **Setup and Deployment** template folder. From the Visual Studio .NET menu bar, choose **File ⇨ Project ⇨ Add New Project**.

2. Select the project type **CAB Project**. Name the project, select the project location, and click the **OK** button. Our example creates a CAB project called **RPressDeployment**. Figure 11.5 displays the **Solution Explorer** pane with the CAB project and associated files.

3.  Right-click the CAB project and choose **Add File**. Select the
    `Manifest.xml` file, the `.dwp` file and the Web Part assembly to be
    included in the CAB file. Our example will include the
    `Manifest.xml` file and the `SiteNav.dwp` file.

4.  Build the CAB project using Visual Studio .NET. The result will be
    a project CAB file located in the output directory for the CAB file
    project. Our example project will create the
    `RPressDeployment.CAB` file in the project output location.

**Figure 11.5:** RPressDeployment CAB Project.

## Install the CAB file using STSAdm.exe

`STSAdm.exe` is a command line utility that performs many administration
functions, including adding, deleting, and enumerating Web Parts installed into
the Virtual Server Gallery. Installing the CAB file on the WSS or SPS server
will install the Web Part's assemblies, resources, definition file, and **SafeControl**
entries. The definition files will be installed into the Virtual Server Gallery.

*Tech Tip:*

STSAdm.exe **is located at** `<root>\Program Files\Common Files\Microsoft Shared\web server extensions\60\bin`. **Instead of typing this long path every time a Web Part is to be added or deleted, consider creating a batch file that sets the correct path to the executable.**

To install the CAB file on the WSS or SPS server, open the command prompt and use the **addwppack** operation of the STSAdm.exe tool to add a Web Part definition to the Virtual Server Gallery by typing the following command:

```
STSAdm -o addwppack  -url <server url> -filename <filename and path>
```

The **–url** argument is used to specify a single virtual server.

Figure 11.6 shows the command to install the **RPressDeployment** CAB file.

**Figure 11.6:** Deploying to the Virtual Server Gallery.

The Web Part has now been deployed to the Virtual Server Gallery and is available for users to search and browse in the tool pane. The `.dwp` file is now installed at `<virtual server root>\wpcatalog`. This file can be opened with Notepad to see that it is indeed the file created in the Web Part project. A look in the `web.config` file will reveal a **SafeControl** element for the Web Part as listed in the `Manifest.xml` file.

## Deleting a Web Part Definition from the Virtual Server Library

You can use the **deletewppack** operation in `STSAdm.exe` tool to delete a Web Part definition from the Virtual Server Gallery. The required argument is –**name**, which is the name of the installed CAB file. Use the –**url** argument to specify a single virtual server. Deleting a Web Part from the Virtual Server Gallery will remove the definition file, the **SafeControl** element in the `web.config` file, and the Web Part assemblies.

To delete a Web Part definition file from the Virtual Server Gallery, you will use the **deletewppack** operation of the `STSAdm.exe` tool.

At the command prompt, run the `STSAdm.exe` tool using the following command:

```
STSAdm -o deletewppack -url <server url>  -name <installed CAB file>
```

Any Web Part page that contains a Web Part defined in the deleted CAB file will return an error.

Figure 11.7 shows the command to delete the **RPressDeployment** CAB file.

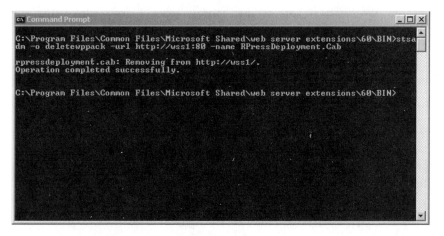

**Figure 11.7:** Deleting the Web Part Definition from the Virtual Server.

**FREE** *Bonus:*

There is another option for installing and deploying Web Parts: the **WPPackager** tool. For information on using the **WPPackager** tool, see the bonus Chapter 12, available after you register this book online at www.rationalpress.com.

# Did you know?

Did you know that external resources like images, XML files and cascading stylesheets can be installed using the `STSAdm.exe` tool?

External resources can be added to the CAB file and installed with a Web Part. The bonus Chapter 13 has more information on how to deploy online resources with the `STSAdm.exe` tool.

# Extras

# Appendix A

# Web Part Life Cycle

A Web Part has a definite start and end state during each request. Web Part developers can handle events fired by the Web Part infrastructure, by the base **WebPart** class, and by ASP .NET. Understanding when and in what order these events occur is important when creating a Web Part. The Web Part examples in this book have shown the use of the **RenderWebPart** method to send content to the output buffer. In addition, there are events which occur during the Web Part's life cycle for which virtual methods in the **WebPart** base class will be called. Figure A.1 depicts the Web Part life cycle.

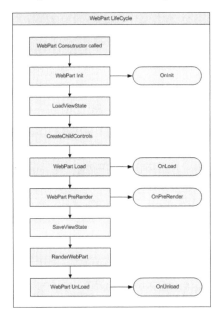

**Figure A.1:** Web Part Life Cycle.

1.  **WebPart Constructor Called** — The new Web Part object is created each time the Web Part page is requested.

2.  **WebPart Init** — The Web Part is initializing. Developers of connected Web Parts can override the **OnInit** method of the **WebPart** class to run custom initialization code.

3.  **LoadViewState** — The **LoadViewState** method is called and the **ViewState** property is restored from the previous **SaveViewState** method. **ViewState** is a property of the base **Control** class that is used to maintain state between requests. Developers can override the **LoadViewState** method of the **Control** class to reconstitute custom objects that were serialized during a previous **SaveViewState** method call.

4.  **CreateChildControls** — The Web Part infrastructure calls the **CreateChildChildControls** method. The **CreateChildControls** method should be overridden and any child controls contained in the Web Part should be created and initialized.

5.  **WebPart Load** — The controls are available, the **ViewState** property has been restored, and the form controls reflect the client state at time of posting. Developers can override the **OnLoad** method to modify the Web Part during this phase. Developers should consider implementing code that is required for each request, such as data source connections in this method.

6.  **WebPart PreRender** — The Web Part is getting ready to render. Asynchronous data fetching (which includes calling the **GetRequiresData** and **GetDate** methods of the **WebPart** class) occurs during this phase. Web Part connections are also created during the **PreRender** phase. Developers can override the **OnPreRender** method to save information to the **ViewState** property during the **PreRenderPhase** phase. ViewState information that is set after the **PreRender** phase will not be available when the Web Part is called back. This means it will not be returned to the client and therefore will not be posted back to the server.

7.  **SaveViewState** — The ViewState information is saved. Developers can override the **SaveViewState** method of the **Control**

class to serialize any complex data that is not easily stored in the **ViewState** property, such as an array of integers.

8. **RenderWebPart** — The Web Part renders content to the output buffer.

9. **WebPart Unload** — The Web Part is unloading from memory. Developers can override the **OnUnload** method to clean up any resources.

The life cycle of a Web Part is basically the same as the life cycle of an ASP .NET **System.Web.UI.Control** object. This should be no surprise, since a Web Part is a type of web control. It is important for developers to understand the basic life cycle phases, and particularly useful to know when the **ViewState** property is restored and available for use. Developers should know at what point in the life cycle the Web Part's control properties reflect the data and state as the WSS or SPS user interface is posted back by the client request. It is also important to understand that the **ViewState** property must be set no later than the **PreRender** phase. Otherwise, the **ViewState** property will not be sent to the client, and any changes to the **ViewState** property made after the **PreRender** phase will be lost. For more information on the **ViewState** property, see Appendix B.

The Web Part shown in figure A.2 will send messages to the **Trace** object as well as to the screen that details the life cycle. See Chapter 7 for information on Web Part tracing.

```
Web Part Life Cycle Demo                                        ▼
8/8/2004 4:05:42 PM - Constructor Called
8/8/2004 4:05:42 PM - OnInit
8/8/2004 4:05:42 PM - OnLoad
8/8/2004 4:05:42 PM - CreateChildControls Called
8/8/2004 4:05:42 PM - CreateChildControls
8/8/2004 4:05:42 PM - OnPreRender
8/8/2004 4:05:42 PM - SaveViewState
8/8/2004 4:05:42 PM - RenderWebPart Called

    Create Post Back
```

**Figure A.2:** Web Part Life Cycle Web Part.

# Did you know?

Did you know that the **SaveProperties** property of the Web Part base class must be set to `true` before the Web Part's **UnLoad** event handler is finished executing or any changed properties will not be saved? The ASP .NET XML serializer will not save the changed properties unless the value of the **SaveProperties** property is set `true`.

# Appendix B

# Using ViewState

**ViewState** is a property of the **Control** class and is a part of ASP .NET that can be used by Web Parts. **ViewState** is used to maintain information between roundtrips from the server to the client. This appendix shows how to add and retrieve stored information from the **ViewState** property.

The **ViewState** property allows the Web Part developer to maintain state in a stateless environment. During a form post, the values of controls in the form are passed to the server. These values are used by the .aspx page to process the form. This ability to store and retrieve information provides the basis for the mechanism which roundtrips the state of a Web Part to the client and back to the server whenever the client requests a post. ViewState information provides a way to maintain state between the client and server for properties and values that are not normally sent back to the server during a post request. This allows Web Parts to reflect the state of the client view on the server site so that processing can continue on the server.

When the ViewState information is moving between the client and server, the **ViewState** property is maintained in a hidden form field named **_VIEWSTATE**. Since the **Microsoft.SharePoint.WebPartPages.WebPart** class inherits from the **System.Web.UI.Control** class, the Web Part can access the base Control's **ViewState** property. The **ViewState** property returns a **System.Web.UI.StateBag** object, which stores data in attribute/value pairs. Developers can add, modify, or remove information from the property bag, which then gets serialized as the hidden **_VIEWSTATE** field and sent to the client. When the form posts back, the **_VIEWSTATE** field is reconstituted as the **StateBag** object and is available to the Web Part during the load event. Prior to the **Load** phase, the **ViewState** property will be empty.

To store a value in the **ViewState** property, use the following syntax:

```
SYNTAX

ViewState[<name>] =
valueViewState["MethodTrace"] =  Message;
// where 'Message' is a string
```

The **StateBag** object actually contains object references and therefore returns an object type that can be cast to the appropriate type. Use the following syntax to access values from the **ViewState** property:

```
SYNTAX



Object = ViewState[<name>]
Message  =  ViewState["MethodTrace"].ToString();
// Again, 'Message' is a string
```

The **Web Part Life Cycle** Web Part discussed in Appendix A uses the **ViewState** property to maintain the trace of the **Web Part Life Cycle** messages as it moves between client and server. The **Web Part Life Cycle** Web Part will store the **LastRenderedTime** value and the **Message** value (both of type **string**) into the **ViewState** property. A postback will *reconstitute* (or *rehydrate*) the ViewState information. The **OnLoad** event handler will "reset" the **LastRenderedTime** and **Message** values. The Web Part will save the **Message** value and update the **LastRenderedTime** and **Message** values to the screen. The Web Part will update the **ViewState** property with the **LastRenderedTime** and **Message** values. The **RenderWebPart** method will output the **LastRenderedTime** and the **Message** values to the screen.

Figure B.1 shows the **Web Part Life Cycle** Web Part after the client has clicked the **Create PostBack** button.

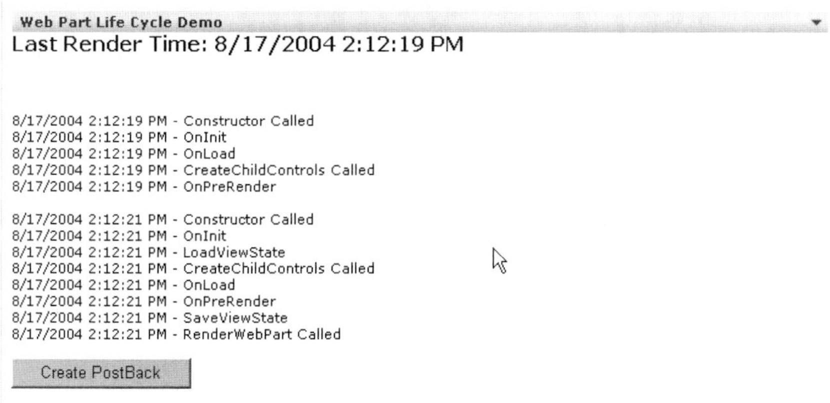

**Web Part Life Cycle Demo**

## Last Render Time: 8/17/2004 2:12:19 PM

```
8/17/2004 2:12:19 PM - Constructor Called
8/17/2004 2:12:19 PM - OnInit
8/17/2004 2:12:19 PM - OnLoad
8/17/2004 2:12:19 PM - CreateChildControls Called
8/17/2004 2:12:19 PM - OnPreRender

8/17/2004 2:12:21 PM - Constructor Called
8/17/2004 2:12:21 PM - OnInit
8/17/2004 2:12:21 PM - LoadViewState
8/17/2004 2:12:21 PM - CreateChildControls Called
8/17/2004 2:12:21 PM - OnLoad
8/17/2004 2:12:21 PM - OnPreRender
8/17/2004 2:12:21 PM - SaveViewState
8/17/2004 2:12:21 PM - RenderWebPart Called
```

Create PostBack

**Figure B.1:** Web Part Life Cycle Web Part Displaying Values Stored in the ViewState Property.

# IMPORTANT NOTICE
# REGISTER YOUR BOOK

## Bonus Materials

Your book refers to valuable material that complements your learning experience. In order to download these materials you will need to register your book at http://www.rationalpress.com.

This bonus material is available after registration:

▶ All code examples in Visual C# .NET and Visual Basic .NET.

▶ Bonus Chapter - Using the WPPackager Tool.

▶ Bonus Chapter - Using External Resources with Web Parts.

▶ Sample Web Parts and Policy File.

## Registering your book

To register your book follow these 5 easy steps:

1. Go to http://www.rationalpress.com.

2. Create an account and login.

3. Click the **My Books** link.

4. Click the **Register New Book** button.

5. Enter the registration number found on the back of the book (Figure A).

6. Confirm registration and view your new book on the virtual bookshelf.

7. Click the spine of the desired book to view the available downloads and resources for the selected book.

**Figure A:** Back of your book.